HORRIBLE SCIENCE

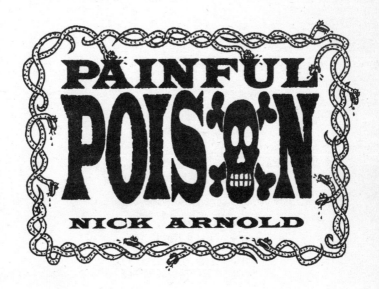

PAINFUL POIS☠N

NICK ARNOLD

Illustrated by
Tony De Saulles

Hippo

Scholastic Children's Books,
Euston House, 24 Eversholt Street,
London, NW1 1DB, UK

A division of Scholastic Ltd
London ~ New York ~ Toronto ~ Sydney ~ Auckland
Mexico City ~ New Delhi ~ Hong Kong

First published in the UK by Scholastic Ltd, 2004

Text copyright © Nick Arnold, 2004
Illustrations copyright © Tony De Saulles, 2004

10 digit ISBN 0 439 97361 9
13 digit ISBN 978 0439 97361 8

All rights reserved

Printed in the UK by CPI Bookmarque, Croydon, CR0 4TD

14 16 18 20 19 17 15 13

The rights of Nick Arnold and Tony De Saulles to be identified as the author and
illustrator of this work respectively has been asserted by them in accordance
with the Copyright, Designs and Patents Act, 1988.

Contents

Nick Arnold has been writing stories and books since he was a youngster, but never dreamt he'd find fame writing about poison. His research involved turning a teacher into a zombie and testing the vomit goblet and he enjoyed every minute of it.

When he's not delving into Horrible Science, he spends his spare time eating pizza, running and thinking up corny jokes (though not all at the same time).

Tony De Saulles picked up his crayons when he was still in nappies and has been doodling ever since. He takes Horrible Science very seriously and even agreed to make friends with a black widow spider. Fortunately, he has made a full recovery.

When he's not out with his sketchpad, Tony likes to write poetry and eat licorice, though he hasn't written any poetry about licorice yet.

INTRODUCTION

BEWARE! I'm worried that this horrible book could be too scary for you!

But this book's about poison and lots of people think poison is a scary subject. Especially if they drink poison by mistake – now that would be DEAD SCARY!

OK – but I have to warn you that this book is more scary than a chemistry class and more terrifying than a terrible test. In fact when we tried to measure how frightening this book was, the machine blew up!

So it's sure to send shivers down your spine. Won't that put you off?

Yes, but this book is about the sick secrets of killer chemicals and the painful effects of drinking them. And it tells you which poisons turn people pink or blue or yellow and all about poisonous plants, snakes, spiders and other cruel creatures…

And then there's the *seriously* sickening stuff like how to turn your sister into a mummy … while she's still alive!

But I really shouldn't be telling you all this…
Maybe I should take this book away?

Oh well, read on if you think you're brave enough. BUT DON'T HAVE NIGHTMARES!

KILLER CHEMICALS

Let's start with a *seriously* scary fact. The whole world is oozing and dripping and squelching with poisons…

• There are poisonous gases.

• And poisonous plants.

• And poisonous animals.

MR STINKS THE CHEMISTRY TEACHER

But what is a poison? Well, read on – you're about to find out!

So what *is* a poison?
A poison is a substance that upsets the chemical workings of your body. To show you what I mean let's

turn Mr Stinks into a giant test tube and check out what's going on inside him… Like any other human body, Mr Stinks' test-tube body is fizzing with billions of chemical changes (or "reactions" as scientists call them).

But poisons mess up these crucial chemical changes. You can imagine a chemical reaction as kids playing a playground game. It might look like chaos, but the game has rules and everyone has a part to play. A poison is like a gang of bullies rampaging through the playground. The bullies chase away the other kids and take over the game and play it to rules that they make up themselves.

In other words, pesky poisons ruin reactions!

So why is a poison deadly?

Without chemical reactions the poor old body can't stay alive. Let's just take another peek at Mr Stinks. He needs chemical reactions every time…

• His brain sends signals to his muscles.

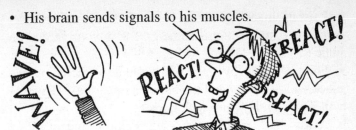

• His muscles move when and where he wants them to.
• His guts digest his food.
• His body makes energy using sugar from his food and oxygen from the air. (The body needs energy to stay alive and power more chemical reactions.)

But if these chemical reactions get messed up by a poison, they may not happen. And Mr Stinks' body may not work properly – it might even die…

The lethal low-down on types of poison
Now, as I said, the world's full of poisons – here are some of the main types…
• Poisonous gases such as carbon monoxide and chlorine – pages 47 and 52 will leave you breathless.
• Poisonous metals such as lead and mercury. You can dig them up on pages 61 and 65 – but don't take a *shine* to them!
• Poisonous substances called metalloids – these include arsenic and antimony. They're on pages 72 and 69, but don't forget your sick bag!

• Poisons made by plants such as deadly nightshade. You can gasp at the gruesome greens in your garden on page 81.
• Poisons made by bugs and animals – including the black widow spider and the green mamba snake. Page 94 will have you howling with horror.
• Acids like nitric acid (see below) and alkaline chemicals such as drain cleaner. These are so strong they can actually dissolve you. Page 128 is fizzing with facts.

Of course, some poisons have even more horrible effects than others…

• Phosphorus (page 68) makes poo and sick glow in the dark.
• Nitric acid causes white frothy snot, burning pain and other effects too revolting for a respectable book like this. Victorian doctors used watered-down nitric acid as an anti-itching lotion – what I call a loopy lotion notion!
• Sodium nitrite stops the blood from taking up oxygen. Oxygen gives the blood its cheerful red colour and without it the body turns bright blue.

But before we go any further there are some people you must meet – you might have seen them on the cover of this book. They're our very own poison experts, Count Orlando Vomito and his assistant Donna Venoma…

BEWARE! SOME INFORMATION ABOUT POISON IS HARD TO SWALLOW!

AND YOU NEED GUTS TO TAKE IT IN!

So what's your favourite poison, Count?

I DON'T HAVE A FAVOURITE. THERE ARE MANY DIFFERENT KINDS AND I LOVE THEM ALL!

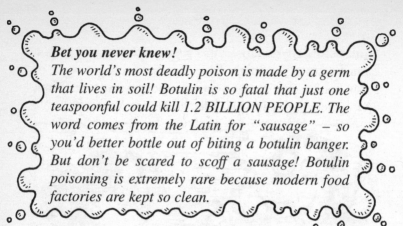

A surprising and scary fact about poisons

Don't panic! Are you sitting calmly? Good – I don't want to worry you but you probably eat and drink poisons regularly! In fact, I'm sure you had some today! I said, DON'T PANIC! Your lunch didn't kill you, did it? These chemicals are only poisonous if you have too much of them at once…

SCHOOL DINNER – REVOLTING BUT NOT POISONOUS

1 Water is a poison! If you drink too much of it you upset the chemistry of your nerve signals. You feel confused and tired and can't stay awake. Death can follow. But don't worry – feeling like this on a Monday morning is nothing to do with the glass of water you drank on

Sunday night! Water is only poisonous if you slurp huge amounts in a few hours.

I HOPE YOU'RE NOT PLOTTING ONE OF YOUR "DAY-OFF-SCHOOL" SCAMS!

2 Salt contains not one but *two* poisons – sodium and chlorine. The poisons are bound together in the salt like two tied-up bullies.

WE'RE A BIT TIED UP AT THE MOMENT...

...AND IT'S A REAL BIND

But if you ate too much salt (and we're talking about quite a few tablespoonsful) it could upset the working of your nerves, with fatal results.

3 Sugar is a poison! It draws water from your body bits into your blood. And when your poor old body tries to get rid of the sugar by weeing, it dries out even more. Sugar can dry out a microbe and shrivel its slimy little body. But DON'T PANIC – since you're a lot bigger than a microbe, you'd need to scoff LOADS of sickly sugary sweets before you suffer this fate…

To find out how much sugar is poisonous let's spoil a teacher's day armed only with a sticky bun and a sickly smile…

Teacher's tea-break teaser

You will need:

A sticky bun

A sickly smile

Knock politely on the staffroom door. Smile sweetly and offer your teacher the sticky bun. (Make sure you haven't taken a bite out of it first.) When your teacher bites the bun, you say…

Take a few moments to enjoy the sight of your teacher turning green and clutching their throat … and then explain that the bun contains sugar which can poison you.

And if you're feeling kind you can go on to explain that you need to eat an awful lot of sugar before it kills you. I mean your teacher would have to scoff about 100 sticky buns before they suffered the full fatal effects. And NO, you can't add 200 tablespoonfuls of sugar to your teacher's tea (or any other substance, including salt or anti-constipation pills). And if you do, you'll probably get extra science homework for life … in prison!

HORRIBLE HEALTH WARNING!

NEVER try poisons or give them to anyone else — ever! Poisons can kill people and people who mess with poisons are dead stupid … and sometimes end up stupidly dead.

How NOT to get poisoned!
Poisons are only deadly if they get into your body – and that means you're safe as long as you DON'T…

Eat or drink a poison. GULP!

Breathe or sniff it in. SNIFF!

Inject it into your blood. SQUIRT!

Touch it (some poisons can soak through the skin). DIP!

Bet you never knew!
In Denmark in 2000 a gang of girls sneaked into a toilet to sniff butane gas. These girls had the brain power of an absent-minded woodlouse. Butane is a poisonous gas used for cooking, so it burns easily. Guess what happened when one of the girls lit a cigarette?

KABOOM!

Well, what do you expect? Smoking is BAD for you! And the girls were smoking non-stop after they caught fire. As I said, taking poison is stupid and those girls were playing with fire.

But no matter how sensible you are, accidents can happen

And if they do I bet you'll be glad you read this next bit about what to do if someone gets poisoned. But before you start, I'd like to say a BIG thank you to our guests, New York private eye MI Gutzache and his faithful dog, Watson.

MI Gutzache has agreed to act the part of a poisoned person. Don't worry, Watson, he's just pretending!

IF THE PERSON ISN'T AWAKE...

1 Can you see what they've taken? Look for poison bottles, half-eaten food, etc. Are there any stains on their skin or clothes?

2 Dial 999 FAST and tell the experts what's happening. Take their advice.

3 Check the person's mouth for bits of food or false teeth or anything that might make them choke.

YUK!

HEY, I AIN'T GOT NO FALSE TEETH!

4 Put them in the recovery position ... like this."

5 Make sure they're warm and comfortable.

OK, MR GUTZACHE, YOU CAN GET UP NOW. MR GUTZACHE?!

ZZZZZZ

Hmm – looks like we've made him a bit *too* warm and comfortable!

IF THE PERSON IS AWAKE...

1 Ask them what they've taken and how much.

2 Dial 999 FAST and tell the experts what's happening. Take their advice.

3 The poisoned person should see a doctor as soon as possible...

NURSE-GET THE STOMACH PUMP!

YIKES!

The doctor treating Gutzache is our medical expert for this book – Dr Grimgrave. Just don't try to make Dr G laugh – he hasn't got a sense of humour!

Doctors often give poisoned patients a substance called activated charcoal to soak up poisons in the stomach. But Dr G is using a stomach pump to suck up poisoned sick … DON'T TRY THIS AT HOME – and definitely not at mealtimes!

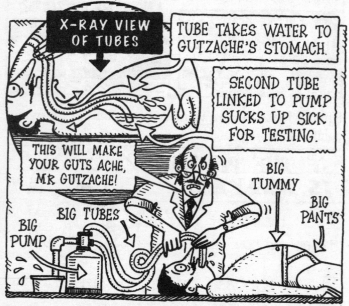

X-RAY VIEW OF TUBES

TUBE TAKES WATER TO GUTZACHE'S STOMACH.

SECOND TUBE LINKED TO PUMP SUCKS UP SICK FOR TESTING.

THIS WILL MAKE YOUR GUTS ACHE, MR GUTZACHE!

BIG TUMMY

BIG PANTS

BIG TUBES

BIG PUMP

Having your stomach pumped out sounds like a painful experience, but I promise you it's NOTHING compared to being poisoned! And I know what that's like because I've been peeping at the next chapter. You'll need real GUTS to read on!

PAINFUL POISON PANGS

OUCH! *ERK!*

Count Vomito is keen to show us the effects of some of his rather large collection of poisons. And that's handy because this chapter is all about what poisons do to the body. All we need is a volunteer to test them on...

HEY, WHY IS EVERYONE LOOKING AT ME?

And now it's time for some sickeningly scary secrets about how poisons work...

How do different types of poison work?

WARNING! SCIENTIFIC WORDS COMING UP!

You'd best close your eyes if you don't want to get blinded by science! Sorry, readers, in order to answer this question, we need to check out a few scientific words. (Mind you, with word-power like this you can sound off like a brainy boffin.)

The PROTEIN MOLECULES and ENZYMES in my CELLS contain millions of ATOMS!

YOU'RE TOO BRAINY FOR THIS SCHOOL, SIMPKINS!

Nearly all the science words you need to make sense of this book

ATOMS – Tiny blobs of matter that make up everything, including you.

MOLECULE – A group of atoms that join up to make up a chemical. It's a bit like you hanging out with your mates at school.

PROTEIN (pro-teen) – A type of molecule found in living things.

ENZYME (en-zime) – A type of protein that speeds up chemical reactions in the body. Without them the body's chemical reactions would be too slow to keep you alive.

CELLS – Your body is made up of billions of microscopic cells…

And here's how poisons work…

1 Some poisons, such as cyanide (see page 92), block key enzymes, so the body dies.

2 Nerve poisons mess up nerve messages from your brain to your muscles. So vital orders such as "KEEP BREATHING" don't get through. Evil examples include nerve gas (page 54).

3 Some poisons dissolve body bits. These poisons are either acid like sulphuric acid (found in car batteries), or alkaline such as oven cleaners (see page 129).

4 And then there's irritant (irr-rit-tant) poisons. These poisons are irritating, like a little brother (only much more so). Irritating brothers make you feel sore and drinking irritant poison can make your guts sore and your stomach vomit. One especially irritating poison is arsenic (see page 72 for the painful particulars).

5 Narcotic (nar-kot-tick) poisons such as morphine (mor-feen) knock the victim out. But some, like strychnine (strick-neen) (see page 90), also have a nasty irritant effect or poison the nerves into the bargain. So the poor poisoned person gets double the trouble!

BIG PROBLEMS for little animals

But the way a poison works doesn't just depend on what poison it is. The amount of poison you've taken is also vital. Or to be more exact – how much you've taken *compared to your size.*

If you wanted to poison an elephant with a poisoned bun, you might need a bun the size of a football. But you can murder a mouse with a bun no bigger than a sugar lump. And to prove this point, the Count has set up an evil experiment involving MI Gutzache, an over-friendly fly and a container of fly spray…

I HAVE RIGGED THE FLY SPRAY SO IT SPRAYS BACKWARDS…

HEE HEE!

PSSSS!

ERK!

BURST

FORTUNATELY, GUTZACHE ISN'T KILLED. ALTHOUGH HE'S HIT BY ENOUGH FLY SPRAY TO KILL A FLY, HE WEIGHS 100,000 TIMES MORE THAN A FLY SO IT WOULD TAKE 100,000 TIMES MORE POISON TO FINISH HIM OFF.

The body strikes back

And now we've sorted out how poisons can affect the body – let's check out how the body defends itself. Can it protect itself at all? Well, you'll be pleased to know the body's got a few secret plans...

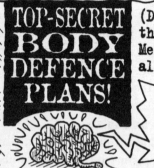

TOP-SECRET **BODY DEFENCE PLANS!**

(Don't let a poisoner see this on pain of death!) Message from the brain to all body bits... °°°○

IT'S DEATH IF WE CAN'T GET RID OF POISON, SO MAKE SURE YOU KNOW OUR PLANS OF ACTION!

IMPORTANT WARNING!

These plans only work with small amounts of not totally deadly poisons such as antimony or arsenic. If there's lots of poison our defences will be overwhelmed. And if the poison's deadly enough to kill in minutes there won't be time to go through all our plans! Go straight to PLAN F!

PLAN A
The body eats or drinks some poison. The stomach and guts try to clear the poison by vomiting and diarrhoea. If the poison gets from the guts into the blood, try...

SPLURB!

BLURRRRRGH!

PLAN B

We can get rid of some poisons straight away by weeing. And it might be worth giving Plan C a go...

PLAN C

Sweat the poison out through the skin. This plan is especially useful for poisons injected into the blood by snakes or spiders. Trouble is if we sweat and wee too much we'll be drying out and dying out! Hmm – looks like we could use some help and luckily there's still Plan D.

SPLOOSH!

BZZZZZZ!

PLAN D

The liver to the rescue! Yes, the liver can get rid of poisons if anything can! Well, let's hope so because...

URRGH!

LIVER

STOMACH

INTESTINES

PLAN E

Er – there isn't one.

PLAN F

PANIC!!!!!!

Now I bet you'd love to read how your life-saving liver can rescue you from a painful poisoning peril. Well, here's your chance...

Painful poison fact file

NAME: The life-saving liver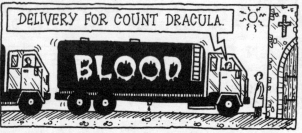

THE BASIC FACTS: **1** Your liver weighs as much as a bag and a half of sugar (about 1.5 kg) and snuggles under your ribs on the right side of your body.

2 The liver is like a sieve filtering your blood. In just five minutes it can filter all the blood in your body. In a year it filters enough blood to fill 23 milk tankers.

DELIVERY FOR COUNT DRACULA.

BLOOD

3 What the liver's after is vital chemicals you need to stay alive – such as vitamins. But it also filters out harmful poisons and treats them chemically to make them safer.

4 Some poisons are sent to the kidneys in the blood and got rid of in wee. Other poisons are chucked out in a digestive juice called bile. They end up in poo.

SO MAKE SURE YOU WASH YOUR HANDS PLOPERLY!

24

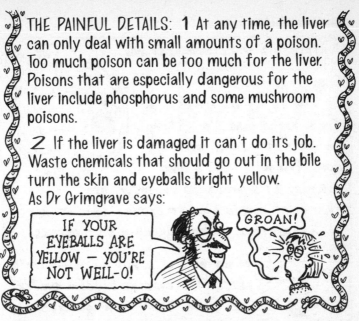

THE PAINFUL DETAILS: 1 At any time, the liver can only deal with small amounts of a poison. Too much poison can be too much for the liver. Poisons that are especially dangerous for the liver include phosphorus and some mushroom poisons.

2 If the liver is damaged it can't do its job. Waste chemicals that should go out in the bile turn the skin and eyeballs bright yellow. As Dr Grimgrave says:

IF YOUR EYEBALLS ARE YELLOW – YOU'RE NOT WELL-O!

GROAN!

Remember how those lovely useful substances like water and sugar can be poisons if you take too much? Another too-much-of-a-good-thing chemical is vitamin A. You can find vitamin A in fish, eggs, butter, milk and carrots. And since it's stored in the liver – guess where else you can find it!

DUH, THE LEG?

ER, THE EARS?

MY NOSE?

That's right, in *liver!* Without the vital vitamin you suffer from skin problems and poor eyesight in the dark. But if you have too much, it can *kill.* Australian explorer Douglas Mawson found this out the hard way. Here are the letters he might have written to his girlfriend…

Antarctica ~ 20 November 1912

WE ARE HERE!

Dear Paquita,
So how is my darling? I'm fine. Right now I'm sitting in my snug tent with my good friends, Mertz and Ninnis. It's great to think we are the first people ever to explore this corner of Antarctica. We're making good progress!

SNOW CRACK!
ICE

Mind you, it's not easy. There's lots of crevasses hidden under the snow. They're huge cracks in the ice hundreds of metres deep, so we'll have to tread carefully! I guess you won't be reading this letter until next year when we get back to Australia - and by then we'll be getting married. I can't wait! Lots of love,

BRRR!

Douglas

Antarctica ~ 13 December 1912

ARGH!

Dear Paquita,
Terrible news! Ninnis has fallen into one of those dreadful crevasses.

With Ninnis went the sledge carrying most of our food and equipment and the dogs that were pulling the sledge.

We spent the whole day calling into the crevasse, listening for a faint cry for help. But we heard nothing – Ninnis must be dead. At least we've still got one sledge and its dogs. If we ration our remaining food, eat the dogs one by one and feed the rest of the dogs on the bones, we might make it back to camp ... just. Here's hoping!

Love,
Douglas

PS Mertz says, "Glad you're not here!"

Antarctica ~ 1 January 1913

Dear Paquita,
I wanted to write to you at Christmas but I've not been feeling too good. We've been eating the dogs and we're down to our last huskie. Dog meat is vile – especially the paws and maybe it doesn't agree with us. Mertz is even worse than me, but you'll be

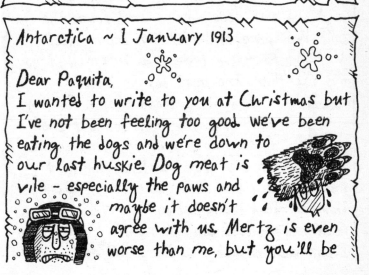

pleased to hear I'm giving him the
best meat - the liver.
Lots of love,

Douglas YUM YUM!

I don't care where I am any more
15 January 1913

SKIN NOT SNOW!

Dear Paquita,
Perhaps this letter will
be found on my frozen
body. By 6 January
Mertz felt worse. We
both had gut pains.
Our skin peeled, our hair was dropping
out and our toes were numb from the
cold. We were still 160 km from safety,
but Mertz had a fever and he couldn't go
any further. The next day he died.
I built a tomb of ice for my
friend. My feet had lost their
skin so I put on extra socks.
Every step hurt. In the next
few days I didn't know whether I was
alive or dead - and I didn't care. I
walk and walk. I don't know if
I can walk much further."

GASP!

Will we ever meet again?
Love you for ever!
Douglas

Antarctica
8 February 1913

SHIVER!

Dear Paquita,
You'll never guess what
happened! Somehow I found
my way to an ice cave
where I knew some food was
stored. Outside a storm raged.
I couldn't leave the cave even though the
camp was just 8 km away! At last the storm
cleared and I set off. I stumbled over a
rise and saw the camp ... and the ship
sailing away. I stared
after it in horror. They've
given up waiting, I
thought. If they don't
come back I'm a dead man...
I staggered into the empty camp. I gazed
about me in despair and that's when I saw
the men who had stayed behind to wait. I
looked so bad they didn't know who I was!
When I looked in the mirror I didn't know

29

who I was either. I look
like a scruffy, skinny,
smelly scarecrow. Worse,
I'm as bald as an egg!

See you soon!
Love,
Douglas

♥ YOU!

PS If you don't want to marry me any
more, I'll understand!

The hero's return

You'll be delighted to know that Douglas Mawson and the other men were able to call the ship back by radio. He returned to Australia a hero and Paquita still wanted to marry him…

But what was the mystery illness that killed Mertz and almost destroyed Mawson? Although no one knew it at the time, they'd been poisoned … by liver. The dogs were Arctic huskies. Like most Arctic animals they store huge amounts of vitamin A in their livers. Enough to cause gut pain, sickness, skin and hair loss if you ate it. Easily enough to kill a man.

Douglas Mawson was the lucky one – he lived because he didn't eat too much liver. And at least his story had a happy ending. Unlike the terrible tales in the next chapter…

If there's one thing more scary than poison, it's a horrible human armed with a poison. Here are some painful tales of how people have used poison.

Thousands of years ago, and no one knows quite when, humans learnt to use poisons for weapons. Native peoples as far apart as Japan, South Africa and South America used poisoned weapons for hunting.

The ancient Greeks knew about poisoned arrows and how poison can get through the skin. In one of the legends about Hercules, the Greek superhero and strong man gets killed by a poisoned vest. The Roman poet Ovid put it a bit more bloodily...

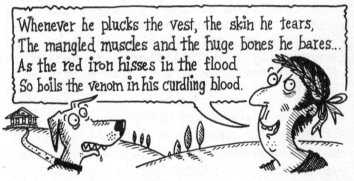

Whenever he plucks the vest, the skin he tears,
The mangled muscles and the huge bones he bares...
As the red iron hisses in the flood
So boils the venom in his curdling blood.

What a great poem! Why not read it in an English class and watch your teacher run out of the room with her hand over her mouth! (By the way, venom is a poison made by an animal.)

Understandably Hercules decided the only way to stop the pain was to burn himself alive – which he did with the aid of a friend. But all wasn't lost, because the gods let him into heaven where he married a goddess. So that's all right then...

Although the story of Hercules is just a story, the ancient Greeks and Romans knew lots about how to poison people. Here's just one case from thousands…

POISON MURDER CASE FILE

VICTIM'S NAME: Agathocles
JOB: King of Syracuse
DATE: 289 BC
PLACE: Sicily
POISONED BY: His grandson
HOW POISONED: He was using the pointy tip of a feather to clean bits of food from between his teeth. But the king's wicked grandson had dipped the feather in poison. The poison stopped the king from moving (it might have been a type of nerve poison).
Everyone thought the king was dead so he was given a traditional ancient Greek funeral. His body was burned — but he was *still alive!*

In those early days the most deadly poisons often came from plants. One popular plant poison was hemlock. In 399 BC Greek philosopher-teacher Socrates (469–399 BC) was sentenced to drink hemlock for "corrupting the youth of Athens". The poison seemed to creep up his body, as his pupil Plato recalled…

The teacher lay down. The man with the poison squeezed his foot. Socrates said he felt nothing. He said that when the poison reached his heart he would be gone.

But all the time he was awake and his thoughts remained clear. Perhaps that's the cruellest thing about hemlock poisoning.

Bet you never knew!
There's no point in daydreaming that your teacher will drink poison. No, it's already happened! In 1928, Hungarian teacher Leo Bruck was teaching his pupils about the death of Socrates. To show what happened he drank some poison ... and died. While we all like teachers who liven up lessons, this could be going a bit too far!

Poisons were often used to bump off important people. In sixteenth-century Italy poisoning was so common that some people killed people for a living!

POISON MURDER CASE FILE

VICTIM'S NAME: Bianca Capello
JOB: Poisoner
DATE: Sixteenth century
PLACE: Florence, Italy
POISONED BY: Herself
HOW POISONED: She was trying to poison Cardinal Ferdinand with a rather tempting poisoned tart. But the clever cardinal switched the sweets and Bianca bumped herself off by mistake.

By Bianca's time, poisons had even become fashion items... We'll be back after the commercial break. Don't go away!

COUNT VOMITO'S POISON PRODUCTS

proudly present...

The Fatal Fashion Poison Jewellery Catalogue

Why not order the latest in our range of delightfully deadly designer jewellery? You can poison your enemies whilst looking really glitzy! IT'S FASHION TO DIE FOR! Everything the well-dressed poisoner needs, including...

POISON RINGS

Store the poison in your ring and put a few drops in your enemy's drink. It's guaranteed to break the ice at parties!

POISON NECKLACES

Supplied complete with a little locket and some poison to put in it. All poison is guaranteed 100% deadly and if you get caught you can always try it on yourself. Satisfaction guaranteed or your money back (if you're still alive, that is!).

ROMANTIC ROSARY PEA NECKLACES

Tasteful black and orange colour to go with your favourite outfit!

MUST NOT SWEAT... MUST NOT SWEAT...

∼∽∽∽∼ THE SMALL PRINT ∼∽∽∼
This necklace is made out of poisonous rosary peas.
So don't sweat when you wear the necklace or the poison
(abrin) can pass into your skin and cause violent stomach
pains. And if you chew the necklace, you'll soon be
resting in peas, I mean, resting in peace.

With so many pesky poisoners about, powerful rulers were dead scared of poison and some were mad scared of it... Sultan Abdul Hamid of Turkey (1842–1918) was especially nervous:

• He only drank water from a secret spring.
• His cow had its own bodyguard to protect its milk.

COWARD

COW

THIS IS **UDDERLY** RIDICULOUS!

• He would only touch food if it had been tested on his food taster AND a cat or a dog.
• He would only put on clothes if they had been tried on by a slave to make sure there was no poison on them.

• His palace was surrounded by a town where 20,000 spies lived. The spies had to spy on each other and make sure none of them were plotting to poison the scared sultan. And just in case the spies didn't spy hard enough there were thousands of parrots – they had to squawk if they saw strangers sneaking about.

You might like to know that awful Abdul was eventually kicked out by the Turkish people when they got tired of his weird ways – but at least he wasn't poisoned!

What these rattled rulers really required was some remedy for poison. But what?

Painful expressions

A scientist says: Do you say…?

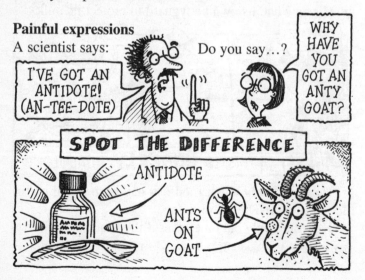

NO, he said DOTE, not *goat*! An antidote is a substance that stops a poison. Mind you, goats did feature in early antidotes, as you're about to find out…

Amazing antidotes

The antidote molecules stick to the poison molecules and stop them doing any harm in the body. Just imagine the poison as a nasty gang of kids looking for trouble. The antidote is a group of nice kids who stick close to the nasty kids to stop them getting into mischief.

In their desperate search for antidotes, important people tried all kinds of weird and wonderful stuff. Do you think either of these would actually work?

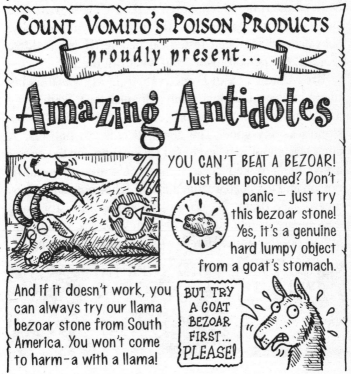

COUNT VOMITO'S POISON PRODUCTS

proudly present…

Amazing Antidotes

YOU CAN'T BEAT A BEZOAR! Just been poisoned? Don't panic – just try this bezoar stone! Yes, it's a genuine hard lumpy object from a goat's stomach.

And if it doesn't work, you can always try our llama bezoar stone from South America. You won't come to harm-a with a llama!

BUT TRY A GOAT BEZOAR FIRST… PLEASE!

37

Still wondering which cure worked? These two true stories will tell you the painful truth. Yes, *both* of these substances have been tested on people. If the antidote worked, the person lived – but what if it didn't?

King Charles IX of France (1550–1574) was thinking of buying a bezoar stone from a Spanish lord. So the king asked his top doctor Ambrose Paré (1510–1590) if the stone was any good. The doctor decided to find out. A cook was about to be executed for stealing and the doctor asked the crooked cook if he would like to swallow poison and the bezoar stone instead. The cook said, "Yes, please." He drank the poison, swallowed the stone and died in agony. The doctor cut open the cook's body and pulled out the stone. Here's what he said to the King…

DO YOU WANT IT?

NO, BURN IT!

Meanwhile in Germany, the curious clay was put to the ultimate test and once again a human life was at stake. I've made up some details, but the basic story is TRUE!

A testing tale
Baden, Germany, 1581

I must die and I know it. I'm a thief – there's no point in denying it now. I've broken the law and I must be hung by the neck until I am dead. And yet … and yet I'm too young to die! I know about medicine. Maybe I'll make a great discovery one day … if I live!

"Mercy!" I beg the judge. "Spare my life – I'll never steal again."

But the old judge shakes his head. "It is the law," he says sternly. "You will die tomorrow."

My heart races and my mouth dries. The guards grab my arms to drag me back to my prison cell. Just then, an idea flashes into my head. It's so strange and so terrible that it seems mad – even to me. But like a drowning boy, I'm clutching at straws…

"Please, please," I whisper. "Grant me one last wish."

"Well?" said the judge. "Make it quick – I haven't got all day."

"Let me take poison. I'll take anything you like…"

"*Poison?*" The judge frowns. "But that will be far more painful than being hung. It will take longer, too. You're not making this easy for yourself, young man!"

"Exactly, but let me also take a little clay. It will be an experiment – and if I die, well, I've saved you the cost of a rope."

The judge whispers to his usher and the public executioner.

Finally, slowly, he nods his head. "Very well," he says. "Have it your own way. You may take mercuric chloride – although I must say you are choosing a worse death for yourself."

Late that night...
I am alone in my cold cell. As I stare at the slimy stone walls I can't get the judge's words out of my head. Tomorrow I must stand in the town square. I will open my lips and drink a tiny spoonful of poison. But that's enough to kill six men – nastily.

I gulp – I try to swallow, but all the muscles of my throat have locked together. I know what the poison can do. I will dribble and throw up and roll around in agony and mess my pants. It could take hours, but I know I'll die in terrible pain.

My only hope is a lump of earth. It's said to help – but no one's ever tested it like this... I don't want to sleep but somehow I doze off in the cold, dark hour before dawn.

The next morning...

It's time. I haven't eaten. Somehow I don't feel like food. Not with my whole body filled with the terror of dying... I am not listening to the court usher's speech... All I see is the small table with a glass of wine, a spoon, a bottle of poison and a small piece of clay. The usher ends his speech with a warning...

"If he lives he will be set free. But if he dies he will not be a pretty sight. You may want to leave now..."

I wish I could leave too.

I gaze blankly at the crowd. They are whispering and shuffling their feet. But no one is leaving.

I stare at the poison in the spoon. It might as well be a sword. The executioner puts the spoon to my lips. I open my mouth and take the poison. I can taste the metal, it burns. I swallow.

The crowd gasps.

I stare at the clay. It's only the size of my thumbnail and it has a goat stamped on it. The executioner drops the clay in the wine and hands me the cup. The pain is worse now. I must swallow the wine fast. Maybe it'll stop the burning…

NO – IT'S NOT WORKING!
The poison is racking me, burning me up inside.
I close my eyes.
I can't …
… stand it …
… any more!
And then …
… somehow the pain is easing. Am I dying? I open my eyes. I am weak and sick. My face is cold and clammy. I take a long ragged breath. It hurts – but I know I'm going to live. The magic clay has saved me.

The clay works like activated charcoal. It soaks up some poisons so that they can't get into the blood. (Actually, charcoal works better than clay.) But there are some poisons for which clay and charcoal are as useless as a bat that's scared of the dark. I'm talking about the grisly, gasping, ghastly poisons in the next chapter…

41

SAFETY WARNING

If you smell something nasty, DO NOT PANIC! The whiff is wafting from your dog or your little brother and NOT this book. If the smell is very bad you may need this item of safety equipment.

IT'S NO CHOKE!

There's something especially scary about poison gas, isn't there? You think the air you breathe will keep you alive – but with poison gas it has the opposite effect. Mind you, you're breathing poison gas at this very moment! *Oh yes, you are!*

Teacher's tea-break teaser

You'll need a large handkerchief and a lot of courage. Knock on the staffroom door and put the hankie to your nose. Your teacher may not be overjoyed to see you after the sticky-bun incident, so smile sweetly and ask them how they're feeling. Your teacher will stare at you suspiciously before muttering, "OK, I suppose." At which point you can say…

Take two seconds to enjoy the look of panic in your teacher's eyes before…

a) Running off at high speed chased by a maddened teacher.

b) Explaining that air contains oxygen – and oxygen is a poison!

Painful poison fact file

NAME: Deadly oxygen

THE BASIC FACTS: **1** Oxygen makes up 21% of the air you breathe. It has no colour, no taste and no smell – but it's there. And you need it to stay alive.

2 Oxygen is breathed in by your lungs and taken on a tour of your body in your blood. It's needed to help your cells make energy.

3 The oxygen you breathe is usually in the form of a molecule made up of two oxygen atoms. To understand how they affect the body, just imagine terrible twins muscling in on playground games and spoiling them.

4 OK, so you'd put up with one set of twins – but not billions of them. Too much oxygen means loads of murderous molecules messing up the vital chemical reactions that keep you going. **BILLIONS**

5 That's why your body puffs out most of the oxygen it breathes in without using it. The oxygen your body does need is locked in red blood cells until it gets to your cells.

THE PAINFUL DETAILS:
1 The first scientist to find out that oxygen was poisonous was French chemist Antoine Lavoisier (1743 – 1794). He put a guinea pig in 100% oxygen … and you can guess the rest.

I'M ABOUT TO USE THIS ANIMAL AS A GUINEA PIG FOR MY EXPERIMENT.

I AM A GUINEA PIG, YOU IDIOT!

2 In 1951 doctors gave tiny newborn babies lots of extra oxygen to help them breathe. But Australian doctor Kate Campbell warned that this was harmful. She was right – the oxygen damaged blood vessels in the babies' eyes and thousands of them lost their sight.

So that's oxygen for you. You can't live without it and you can't live with too much of it! But those naughty oxygen twins also get into the wrong kind of company and make different poison gases. And here are the painful results…

The Gruesome Guide to Poison – Part 1
Gasping Gases

Name: CARBON DIOXIDE

Alias: CO_2 (this is the chemical symbol of the gas)

Description: The terrible oxygen twins plus a new pal - a carbon atom. Together they make a colourless gas that you can't see or smell.

Horrible habits: The count says that breathing in too much carbon dioxide can suffocate the body. He says he's got some spare gas if we want to find out what it's like. Thanks, but no thanks, Count.

Known haunts: Bonfires and coal fires. 0.03% of air is carbon dioxide. When your cells make energy, carbon dioxide is a waste product, which you breathe out.

Redeeming features: Plants love it. They take carbon dioxide from the air and use the carbon atoms to make food. And that means all the fruit and vegetables you eat - including the slimy broccoli you were force-fed for lunch - contain chemicals from a poisonous gas.

BUT I'M GOOD FOR YOU!

<u>Name:</u> SULPHUR DIOXIDE

<u>Alias:</u> SO_2

<u>Description:</u> A smelly gas. Contains the terrible oxygen twins plus one sulphur atom.

<u>Horrible habits:</u> Turns water acid. In the atmosphere it can make rainwater into poisonous "acid rain". When the gas mixes with moisture in the lungs it can make acid lungs too.

<u>Known haunts:</u> Coal smoke, traffic fumes.

<u>Redeeming features:</u> Dissolves boring historic buildings that children get dragged round on school trips. But you like old buildings? Well, cheer up, kids, the gas kills germs too.

BLAST IT! WE'LL HAVE TO TAKE THEM TO *FUN-RIDE PARK*, MISS SIMKINS.

Name: CARBON MONOXIDE

Alias: CO

Description: Just one oxygen on the prowl with its carbon pal. Once again, they're impossible to see or smell but without the second oxygen atom they're worse. Far, far, WORSE!

Horrible habits: They like nothing better than hitching a free ride on board red blood cells and they enjoy the ride so much they don't get off. But that means they take the place of oxygen. With too little oxygen reaching its cells, the body can die.

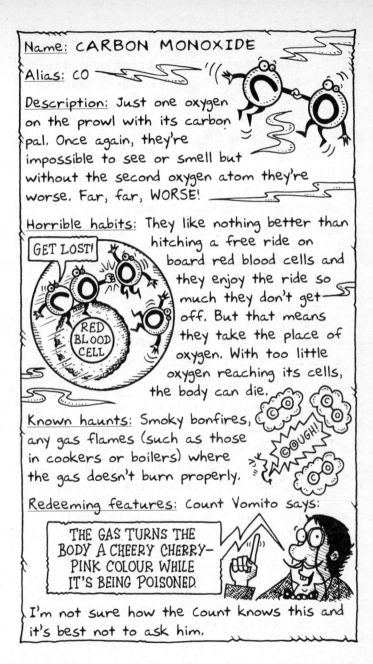

GET LOST!

RED BLOOD CELL

COUGH!

Known haunts: Smoky bonfires, any gas flames (such as those in cookers or boilers) where the gas doesn't burn properly.

Redeeming features: Count Vomito says:

> THE GAS TURNS THE BODY A CHEERY CHERRY-PINK COLOUR WHILE IT'S BEING POISONED.

I'm not sure how the Count knows this and it's best not to ask him.

POISON MURDER CASE FILE

VICTIM'S NAME: Michael Malloy

JOB: Tramp

DATE: 1933

PLACE: New York

POISONED BY: Bar owner Tony Marino, his barman Daniel "Red" Murphy and undertaker Frankie Pasqua.

HOW POISONED: Tony and Frankie were down on their luck. Tony's bar wasn't making too much money and Frankie's funeral business was dying on its feet. So they decided to poison the homeless tramp and claim a big insurance payout. Trouble was the tramp didn't die. They gave him...

● Antifreeze to drink. Malloy glugged it down and asked for more. DON'T TRY THIS AT HOME! Antifreeze is deadly even in small doses.

● Rotten sardine sandwiches and rotten oysters. Malloy asked for seconds.

At last, after failed attempts to run Malloy down and freeze him to death, the gang gassed the tramp with carbon monoxide. But the cops were hearing bad stories about Tony Marino and the boys. So they dug up Malloy's body and its pink colour proved how he'd died. The corpse might have been in the pink but the gang looked a lot less healthy when they were executed the following year.

Carbon monoxide is a real danger, so if you have gas heating or a gas cooker, it's a good idea to pester your parents to get a carbon-monoxide detector. It's a serious matter – but at least poison gases have their funny side. It's true! There's one type that makes you laugh and act rather silly – the Gruesome Guide has the full funny facts…

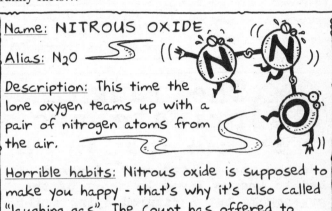

Name: NITROUS OXIDE

Alias: N_2O

Description: This time the lone oxygen teams up with a pair of nitrogen atoms from the air.

Horrible habits: Nitrous oxide is supposed to make you happy - that's why it's also called "laughing gas". The Count has offered to test the gas on MI Gutzache and you can read Gutzache's report on page 50.

THAT'S NOT FUNNY!

Known haunts: Car exhausts ... and thunderstorms. Lightning causes a chemical reaction that combines nitrogen and oxygen in the air to make the gas. But prancing around in a thunderstorm isn't likely to cheer you up. And you definitely won't be smiling if you get struck by lightning!

Redeeming features:
A bit of nitrous oxide relaxes the muscles and lowers the blood pressure. The gas can be mixed with oxygen to numb pain during an operation or when a woman gives birth.

YOU'VE HAD SEXTUPLETS, MRS BROWN!

HA! HA! OOH, DON'T MAKE ME LAUGH, NURSE! HA! HA! HA! HA! HA! HA!

The laughing private eye

REPORT BY MI GUTZACHE

"So the gas is harmless?" I asked. I had to know – I may be short of the greenbacks but I figured dying could be a bad career move.

The Count looked kinda shifty. "It depends on the dose," he said. "Of course we could test how much gas would be fatal."

That was an offer I could refuse but I took the job anyhow. "But just a little sniff," I said. I figured it couldn't do no harm. So I was wrong.

When I sniffed the gas, colours seemed brighter and the ends of my fingers tingled and went numb. And then I got happy – I hadn't felt this happy since I busted Tony "Big Cheese" Mozzarella for the Pasta Poison Plot. Jokes ain't my game but I found myself laughing at some dumb wisecrack the Count made...

WHAT IS DONNA'S JOB?

HUH?

SHE'S MY **POISON-AL** ASSISTANT!

HA HA HA HA HA!

GET A LIFE!

I was laughing so hard I banged my head. But I didn't feel no pain!

IMPORTANT ANNOUNCEMENT

We would like to deny rumours that Horrible Science books have been sprayed with laughing gas in a pathetic attempt (ho ho!) to make you laugh at the painfully corny jokes (giggle, snort). This is a laughable, HA HA HEE HEE! lie. And anyway, someone's already tried it...

Bet you never knew!
In 1996 an Italian club owner was found guilty of pumping laughing gas into his club. Maybe he was trying to make people laugh at his jokes, but the judge didn't see the funny side. The crazy club owner was fined. What's that? You fancy playing a trick like that too? OK, go ahead, just so long as you don't mind losing all your pocket money for the next 2,000 years.

Gruesome poison-gas weapons

One of the best things you can say about nitrous oxide is that it can block pain and save lives. But some scientists have been working to make poison gases that have the opposite effects – poison-gas weapons...

To get an idea how scary poison-gas weapons are, let's join a group of French soldiers. In 1985 they were training to deal with poison gas on the island of Corsica. The soldiers were told a plane would let off steam to give the impression of gas. Sure enough the plane flew over, but the spray was RED – it looked like *real* poison gas! The soldiers fell down and rolled about in agony. But there was no poison and no gas. Someone had simply added red dye to the steam.

These men were big tough soldiers. If they could be terrified by poison gas, what about the rest of us?

Five painful poison gases (in order of nastiness)
5 Chlorine gas

This gruesome yellowish-green gas cloud irritates the lungs. The lungs fill with fluid, and victims drown on dry land. It was first used by the Germans against the French in 1915 during the First World War. Later on in the war, the British used it against the Germans.

Vicious verdict:

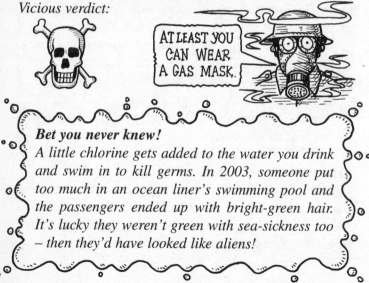

AT LEAST YOU CAN WEAR A GAS MASK.

Bet you never knew!
A little chlorine gets added to the water you drink and swim in to kill germs. In 2003, someone put too much in an ocean liner's swimming pool and the passengers ended up with bright-green hair. It's lucky they weren't green with sea-sickness too – then they'd have looked like aliens!

4 Mustard gas

Used by both sides in the First World War. Causes skin blisters that can rot. Victims can go blind for a short while and suffer damage to their stomach and lungs that can last for years.

Vicious verdict:

Very, *very* nasty. You *must* wear a gas mask, and you can't let the gas touch your skin either. It stays dangerous for weeks, too. On Friday, 13 July 1917, a group of soldiers had mustard gas fired at them for eight hours. The next day their captain said...

Everyone was round the shell holes vomiting ... breathing was very difficult ... as we got going the road seemed to fade away ... (we were) stone blind! I think the worst part was when they opened your eyes to put droplets in them — it was just like boiling water dropping in!

3 Hydrogen cyanide gas
More deadly than chlorine or mustard gas. You feel faint
and weak and throw up. Then you can't breathe, and die.
It only takes a few minutes. It's said to smell of bitter
almonds, although most people can't make out the smell.
By the way, the Count is offering free sniffing sessions if
anyone wants to try… (Don't all rush at once.)
Vicious verdict:

A killer. Although a gas mask will protect you, you have
to keep changing the filter. Luckily the gas blows away
quickly.

2 BZ
An especially revolting weapon. It causes confusion,
diarrhoea and drying of the guts and mouth resulting in
disgusting bad breath. After about 12 hours victims see
things that aren't there and start talking to trees.
Vicious verdict:

A real stinker in more ways than one.

1 Nerve gases
Remember those nasty nerve poisons from page 20?
Nerve gases are the ultimate horror. They're so deadly

that even a few drops on the skin will kill. Victims suffer headaches and throw up and have to go to the toilet in a hurry. They can't stop dribbling and they can't breathe. They die.

Vicious verdict:

What can you say about a gas that makes you need to wear a nappy? The only protection is a hot, clumsy suit that's horrible to wear. But it's less horrible than nerve gas.

Bet you never knew!

The actual use of chemical weapons in war has been banned since 1925 and today many world leaders and scientists would like to get rid of these terrible weapons altogether.

Of course, war always brings out the worst in people, but some people don't need a war to show their worst side. No, I'm not talking about unkind teachers, bullies and the sort of people who complain about children chatting in libraries. I'm talking about people who use poison to kill their enemies, their friends ... and even their pets!

LET'S GET OUTTA HERE!

METALS, MURDER AND MADNESS

QUESTION: What's shiny and cold and passes on electric shocks?

If you said "my dog's nose" then **a)** you really do need to read on and **b)** unplug your puppy from the fairy lights – AT ONCE! The answer is actually – METAL.

Now, you probably know that your home is full of metal things and if you're lucky your pockets are jingling with metal items in the shape of coins. But I bet you never knew there are over 60 types of atom (or elements as a chemist would call them) that happen to be metals. And some are amazingly odd – like caesium (see-zee-um), a metal that burns in air.

But some metals should carry a special health warning…

They can do scarily painful things to the poor human body. And if there's one thing more scary than the metals themselves – it's the fact that some inhuman humans like nothing better than putting them in a cup of coffee.

And here's what makes these murderous metals so dreadfully deadly…

Painful poison fact file

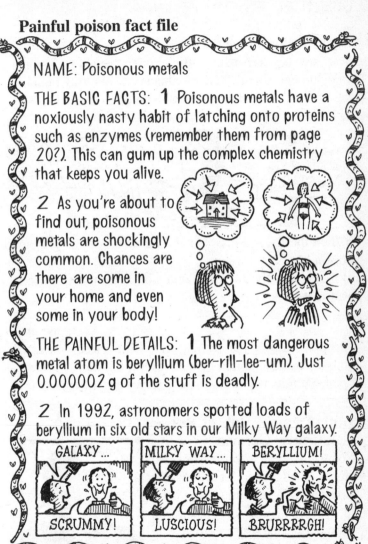

NAME: Poisonous metals

THE BASIC FACTS: **1** Poisonous metals have a noxiously nasty habit of latching onto proteins such as enzymes (remember them from page 20?). This can gum up the complex chemistry that keeps you alive.

2 As you're about to find out, poisonous metals are shockingly common. Chances are there are some in your home and even some in your body!

THE PAINFUL DETAILS: **1** The most dangerous metal atom is beryllium (ber-rill-lee-um). Just 0.000002 g of the stuff is deadly.

2 In 1992, astronomers spotted loads of beryllium in six old stars in our Milky Way galaxy.

GALAXY… SCRUMMY!

MILKY WAY… LUSCIOUS!

BERYLLIUM! BRURRRRGH!

And now you've picked up a couple of nasty nuggets of knowledge about beryllium – can you solve this poison puzzle?

Could you be a scientist?
You are top German boffin Robert Bunsen. You're studying beryllium when a fly lands on your only blob of the stuff … and eats it. What do you do?
a) Eat the fly in a nice ham and mustard sandwich.

BUT I HATE MUSTARD.

ME TOO, BZZZZ!

b) Kill the fly and dissolve and burn its body to get the poison back.
c) Keep the fly as a pet and notice how the poison affects it.

Answer: b) The fly ate the beryllium because it tasted sweet. Although Bunsen wasn't daft enough to eat the fly, he was a really crazy chemist and deserves a place in our…

Hall of Fame: Robert Bunsen (1811–1899)
Nationality: German

Young Robert's professor dad taught languages but brainy Bunsen junior was into chemistry. In fact he was so keen on chemistry that he studied the subject at four universities –

Göttingen, Paris, Berlin and Vienna. He became most interested in cacodyl (ca-co-di-al), an evil-stinking mixture that includes arsenic. The awful arsenic almost bumped off Bunsen and the killer cacodyl blew up, blasting Bunsen with bits of test tube. The scientist went blind in one eye. (And you thought your chemistry lessons were tough!)

Now most sane people would have given up chemistry and taken up something a bit less dangerous, like bungee jumping into volcanoes. But not reckless Robert...

He went on to discover two new elements – the metals caesium and rubidium. And, thank you for asking, he DIDN'T discover the Bunsen burner. It was actually developed by his assistant Peter Desaga in 1855. But Bunsen deserves some credit because he let other scientists copy the idea for free.

Like most crazy chemists Bunsen kept forgetting things (I blame all those poisons). He always forgot the dates of dinner parties and would turn up one day late and expect to be fed. In the end his friends got into the habit of organizing special one-day-late parties just for him. And this may have been a good idea because he was very smelly from all the chemicals he used. The wife of his friend Emil Fischer said:

First I would like to wash Bunsen, then I would like to kiss him because he is such a charming man.

By the way, turning up for school one day late and smelling oddly won't necessarily make you a great scientist! Bunsen was a genuine genius, so he got away with some barmy behaviour.

And now let's get to grips with some more murderous metals ... er, maybe you'd better put some gloves on first...

The Gruesome Guide to Poison – Part 2
Murdering Metals

Name: COPPER

Alias: Cu

Description: A pretty, orangey-pinky, shiny metal (in fact you could even say it's copper-coloured!). Like all metals, copper warms up quickly when you heat it and electricity can run through it easily.

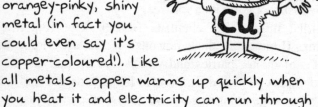

Horrible habits: Too much copper is poisonous.

Known haunts: Copper water pipes, electrical cables and saucepans in posh kitchens.

Redeeming features: Copper atoms help make up some proteins and enzymes - so SHOCK, HORROR! a tiny amount of copper is GOOD for you!

The really seriously sickening stuff isn't actually pure copper, it's copper sulphate. It can be mixed with water to make the sinister blue liquid much loved by science teachers. But don't add copper sulphate to your teacher's tea. The poison causes cramps and a dose of more than 10 grams will kill.

I LOVE IT!

SINISTER SCIENCE TEACHER

And then you'll get collared by the coppers. Mind you, the ancient Egyptians used copper sulphate as an ointment for sore eyes.

Name: LEAD

Alias: Pb

Pb *CLONK!* *ERK!*

Description: A heavy, soft, grey metal. You'd know if you dropped it on your foot, but at least you could take out your rage by bending it into interesting shapes.

Horrible habits: Very poisonous. It can get into the body through the lungs, skin, food and drink. Although the body chucks some of it out in poo, lead can build up in the bones and teeth and other body bits (where it sticks to proteins).

URRRRGH! *KSPLOSH!*

CENSORED
SOMEBODY WITH LEAD POISONING, GETTING RID OF SOME HEAVY POO...

CRACK!

Victims of lead poisoning have...

MADNESS

BELLY ACHE

GROAN, GIBBER!

MUSCLE PAINS AND WEAKNESS

BLUE GUMS

Known haunts: Batteries, soldering (soft metals melted to glue other metals together), hair dye for greying hair (yes, your ageing teachers could have a head full of lead). Lead also lurks in old paint, and in the flashing on the roofs of houses (the metal between the roof and the brickwork). And it was once added to petrol to stop the engine making knocking sounds, but that's now banned in many countries. The one place you WON'T find lead is in pencil "lead". As any clued-up chemist knows that stuff is graphite - so it's all right, you can suck your pencil in a science test and live to tell the tale...

CLEANER FUMES

RATTLE! KNOCK!

DRIBBLE

Redeeming features: Lead has loads of uses, and these days it's kept away from food and drink ... unlike the good old days when your teacher wore short, baggy trousers and got whipped for not doing their science homework. See you after the commercial break...

COUNT VOMITO'S POISON PRODUCTS

proudly present...

The Lethal Lead Experience

Complete with free hospital treatment!

LIVE IN THE PAST WITH THESE GENUINE IMITATION ANTIQUES!

1. Victorian lead pipes for your home – guaranteed to gurgle loudly in the middle of the night!

2. Roman lead boiling pot for sweet wine with a kick!

SUCK! 3. Lead dummies for babies flavoured with rea-tasty lead paint.

IMPORTANT ANNOUNCEMENT
Er, sorry, readers – the Count's just confessed that one of these items is a fake. Which one?

Answers:

1 Genuine.

2 Genuine.

3 FALSE. Huh! As if a parent would let their baby suck lead! No, lead was made into toys such as lead soldiers for older children – and I bet *they* sucked them. Sadly, lead harms the brain and is linked to lower intelligence in children. But talking about lead, I've got a wicked idea for a '"Teacher's tea-break teaser". Will you be "lead" astray?

Teacher's tea-break teaser

You will need:

A pair of running shoes for a speedy getaway

An elderly teacher

Hammer loudly on the staffroom door (elderly teachers can be a little hard of hearing). When your teacher appears, ask them...

DO YOU HAVE ANY LEAD IN YOUR BODY?

If they say "no", you could say...

a) "But there's lead in your hair dye."

b) "What about the wine you drank in Roman times?"

But even lethal lead poisoning isn't as bad as our next murderous metal...

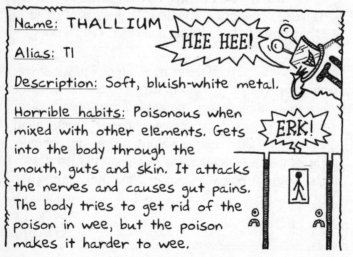

Name: THALLIUM

Alias: Tl

HEE HEE!

Description: Soft, bluish-white metal.

Horrible habits: Poisonous when mixed with other elements. Gets into the body through the mouth, guts and skin. It attacks the nerves and causes gut pains. The body tries to get rid of the poison in wee, but the poison makes it harder to wee.

ERK!

The skin becomes so sensitive it can't be touched and the victim can't smile or change the expression on their face. They lose control of their eyeballs and their hair drops out.

Known haunts: Used in industry.

Redeeming features: It's useful for getting rid of rats.

AND PEOPLE TOO! READ ON...

AND PEOPLE TOO! READ ON...

Bet you never knew!
In 1971, mad poisoner Graham Young tried to poison his work-mates with thallium. He killed two people but gave himself away when some scientists came to investigate the poisonings. Graham seemed to know a lot about poisons and actually asked the scientists if they suspected thallium. As they say, a little learning is a dangerous thing – but that shouldn't put you off reading this book!

Name: MERCURY

Alias: Hg

COOL!

Description: A silvery-grey metal that's runny at room temperature. Like most substances, mercury takes up more space as it warms up, and that's why mercury in a thermometer goes up when it's hot and down when it's cold. And when it's frozen you'd best go to bed and snuggle up with this book.

<u>Horrible habits</u>: Builds up in the body. Damages the brain and kidneys. Bad poisoning results in madness and stops you from weeing. And you end up with yellow skin, black gums and teeth falling out.

BY GUM, I'M FEELING A BIT "DOWN IN THE MOUTH".

<u>Known haunts</u>: Thermometers and industrial chemicals.

<u>Redeeming features</u>: If you can't wee, you won't feel the urge to visit the loo halfway through a long film.

Mind you, this scary horror movie is so gruesome it would make anyone dash for the toilet...

INVASION OF THE METALLOIDS

EEEK!

THEY CAME FROM SPACE TO EAT OUR LAWNMOWERS!

And that's the subject of our next creepy chapter...

INVASION OF THE METALLOIDS

"Metalloids" – they sound like aliens that do terrible things to people involving lots of gagging noises and gory goo. And that's more or less what they do. Fancy finding out a few painful facts…?

Painful poison fact file

NAME: Metalloids. (They're also known as "semi-metals", which doesn't sound quite so sinister even if it does sound a bit odd.)

THE BASIC FACTS: **1** Metalloids are both metals and non-metals at the same time.
2 Confused? Well, a metalloid is an element that has some features of a metal – shiny, lets electricity and heat through, etc – but not all of them!

THE PAINFUL DETAILS: **1** Like poisonous metals, the murderous metalloids featured in this chapter burst into the body like gatecrashers at a party. They bind to proteins and enzymes and stop them doing their jobs. **2** No wonder they were used by some seriously sinister killers!

LET'S PARTY!

The Count has kindly offered to show us the effects of metalloids by testing them on MI Gutzache...

YOU CAN COUNT ME OUT, COUNT!

On second thoughts, maybe it's better if we stick to the Gruesome Guide...

The Gruesome Guide to Poison – Part 3 Mysterious Metalloids

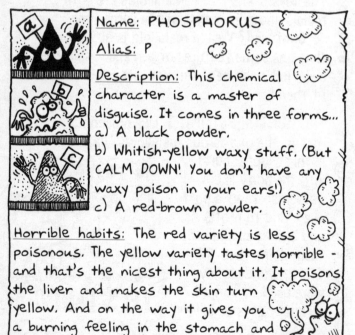

Name: PHOSPHORUS

Alias: P

Description: This chemical character is a master of disguise. It comes in three forms...
a) A black powder.
b) Whitish-yellow waxy stuff. (But CALM DOWN! You don't have any waxy poison in your ears!)
c) A red-brown powder.

Horrible habits: The red variety is less poisonous. The yellow variety tastes horrible - and that's the nicest thing about it. It poisons the liver and makes the skin turn yellow. And on the way it gives you a burning feeling in the stomach and makes your breath smell of garlic.

<u>Known haunts:</u> Fertilizer. Once used for match heads, and rat poison.

<u>Redeeming features:</u> You need phosphorus to stay healthy. Linked up with other chemicals it does no harm in your body. In fact it's used (amongst other things) to build your bones. Mind you, don't eat the pure poison or you'll end up with just bones and no body.

> NOT AGAIN! WHY NOT GERBIL OR HAMSTER POISON?

<u>Name:</u> ANTIMONY

<u>Alias:</u> Sb

<u>Description:</u> Nice shiny look. But no, it's NOT silver, so don't try putting it in your pockets. It breaks easily and it's a poison!

<u>Horrible habits:</u> Antimony can build up in the body until one day you wake up dead. The Count says that victims feel sick, throw up and make lots of extra snot. It's like having bad flu and food poisoning all rolled into one. Oh yes, and you get diarrhoea thrown in for good measure.

69

<u>Known haunts:</u> Used in industry and also some types of enamels and paints.

<u>Redeeming features:</u> If you got poisoned at least you wouldn't have to go to school - maybe not ever!

WORRY!

ER — I THINK WE'D RATHER GO TO SCHOOL!

We'll be back with the most murderous metalloid of all after the commercial break – bye for now!

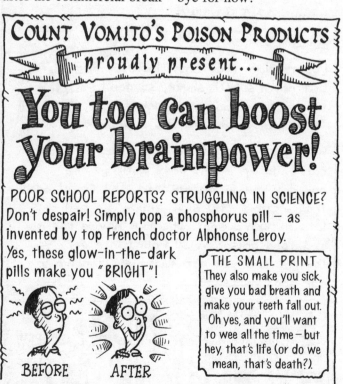

COUNT VOMITO'S POISON PRODUCTS
proudly present...

You too can boost your brainpower!

POOR SCHOOL REPORTS? STRUGGLING IN SCIENCE? Don't despair! Simply pop a phosphorus pill — as invented by top French doctor Alphonse Leroy. Yes, these glow-in-the-dark pills make you "BRIGHT"!

THE SMALL PRINT
They also make you sick, give you bad breath and make your teeth fall out. Oh yes, and you'll want to wee all the time – but hey, that's life (or do we mean, that's death?)

BEFORE   AFTER

GET THIS, GIRLS! ♫ New glow-in-the-dark funky phosphorus skin cream! As worn by Victorian ladies in the 1870s — it gives you a healthy glow when you're "glowing" out clubbing!

VICTORIAN HANDBAGS

THE SMALL PRINT – And it's smelly and damages the skin.

FANCY A BIT MORE ICE CREAM? FEELING A BIT TOO FULL UP?

TOO RIGHT!

Make room for it by drinking from the...

VOMIT GOBLET

One sip and you'll be chucking up all over the carpet! (Made from genuine antimony.)

As used by the Romans so they could eat even more in their giant greedy banquets...

ATE TWO, BRUTUS?

NO, TWENTY, CAESAR... BLEURRRRRGH!

And now, it's time to get a flavour of the most murderous metalloid. Well, maybe getting a "flavour" isn't the best way to put it. And no, Count Vomito, I DON'T want to sample it!

<u>Name:</u> ARSENIC <u>Alias:</u> As

<u>Description:</u> Grey-white and easy to crunch if you chew it, but that's a bit silly.

<u>Horrible habits:</u> Some good news: on its own, arsenic would happily pass through the guts on a one-way trip to the toilet. Some bad news: it's never on its own. For example, it combines with oxygen from the air. And it can get into the body through the mouth or skin, or by being breathed in as a gas.

<u>Known haunts:</u> YIKES! It's EVERYWHERE! There's arsenic in soil, the sea, and not to mention a teeny bit in your body. In tiny doses it's not too bad, but in large doses it's deadly.

<u>Redeeming features:</u> If it wasn't for arsenic, you couldn't play your favourite computer game. Yes, there's arsenic in the semiconductors - vital electrical bits - of a computer.

The effects of arsenic are complicated and painful, so we've asked Dr Grimgrave for an expert medical opinion. Beware – he's in a grumpy mood. Er – come to think of it, he's *always* in a grumpy mood…

THE EFFECTS OF ARSENIC
by Dr H Grimgrave

Arsenic is a fascinating poison because it can affect the body in so many interesting ways.

Sadly I don't see too many of these cases — but if anyone's got any spare poisoned body bits I could do with some for my private medical collection!

A small dose

Arsenic widens blood vessels in the skin and gives it a "glow", as ill-educated persons say. Can you believe some idiots in Victorian times took the poison as a tonic and their idiot doctors encouraged them?! As the poison builds up in the body, the hair and nails fall out and the skin turns yellow from liver damage.

AH YES, YOU'RE LOOKING MUCH BETTER! HAVE ANOTHER BOTTLE!

IDIOT DOCTOR   IDIOT PATIENT

Other problems are weakness, vomiting, diarrhoea, a puffy face, dizziness, sore eyes, nose and mouth. In fact there are enough ailments to keep an overworked doctor like me busy for hours!

A large dose

Patients who have taken a lot of arsenic suffer terrible vomiting and diarrhoea, violent gut pains and death in an hour. I usually see these patients first. Of course one has to make hard choices at times. One idiot who wasn't poisoned at all said he would die in 50 seconds so I told him "Sit down and I'll see you *in a minute,* ha ha!" But I can't sit here blathering all day — I've got some more idiots to see!

73

Now I bet you'd rather share your home with a bad-tempered hippo with bottom problems than a lorry-load of arsenic – but in Victorian times people didn't understand the full dangers of this poison. Let's go and spend Christmas with this typical Victorian family … and their amazing collection of arsenic items!

1. Arsenic paint on wall 2. Arsenic rat poison
3. Arsenic-coated playing cards 4. Arsenic paper to kill flies 5. Arsenic in dye on curtains
6. Arsenic in dye on carpet 7. Arsenic Christmas tree decorations 8. Arsenic wrapping paper
9. Arsenic cloth on card table

Feeling unwell yet? If you're worried about all that nasty arsenic on your fingers, don't try licking it off! NO, why not wash it off with the Victorian family's de-luxe arsenic soap?

Awful arsenic murders

Arsenic has no taste and no smell and since it was easy to buy in shops, the poison was first choice for cruel Victorian killers. Most arsenic murder stories go like this…

Someone dies. The poisoner inherits their money, plus a large insurance payout. Someone else gets suspicious. The body is dug up and arsenic is found. The poisoner gets caught, put on trial and executed. End of story.

But there's one true arsenic murder story that's different. Firstly, it might not have been a murder at all and secondly, the accuser was a ghost! This scary tale from Count Vomito's private poison library is sure to chill your blood…

St John's Church, London, 1850
Mr Graves blew the dust off a coffin lid and squinted at the brass plate. "I fink we've found her, Mr Archer," he called to the young artist.

Archer was perched on a nearby coffin, sketching the ancient crypt with its stone walls and huge dusty cobwebs. Next to him sat Mr Graves's young son, Joe.

"Is your drawing for a book, Mr Archer?" asked Joe. The boy shivered. The winter's night was cold as the grave.

"Yes, Joe. A drawing of Fanny Kent for a book of strange stories."

75

"It's a strange story, right enough," remarked Mr Graves as he rubbed some warmth back into his hands.

"I heard you knew about her," said Archer, without looking up.

"Ho yes, sir, I know everything!" replied Graves. "And if you likes, I can tell you and Joe the 'ole story."

Archer nodded his agreement and Graves sat down heavily. Then he began his tale...

"It happened about 50 years afore I was born. William Kent and his wife, Fanny, came to lodge with Richard Parsons. And that's when it all started. The ghostly knocking and scratching. All night long it went on – a-knocking and a-scratching on the wall."

"It must have been frightening," said Archer.

"I should say so! No one slept a wink. And poor Fanny said it was a sign that she must die..."

"Why did she fink that, Dad?" asked Joe.

"I dunno, son. Maybe she felt unwell or somefink..."

"So who was this ghost?" asked Archer.

"Well, sir. That's the mystery. Some said it was Fanny's sister come to warn Fanny that her husband was poisoning her. He stood to gain £100 in Fanny's will. And there were some what even saw the ghost. They said it was a woman shining so bright you could see your watch by the light! Soon after, the Kents moved out and Fanny died. Mr Kent said it was smallpox wot carried her off, but the ghost told Parsons it was *arsenic*."

"How did it say that? I thought it just made noises," said Archer with a frown.

"Parsons invented a code. One knock for 'yes' and two for 'no'. By now it was the talk of the town. Lords and ladies came to listen to the ghost. And the Lord Mayor asked a group of experts to find out the truth."

"And did they?" asked Archer.

"They found out the ghost didn't knock unless Parson's little girl was around. And it didn't knock when the girl was watched closely. Some days before the experts arrived, the ghost had said it would knock on Fanny's coffin. So the experts came to this very spot and called out, 'ARE YOU THERE, FANNY KENT?' … but nuffink happened."

All at once something bumped in the shadows. Joe nearly jumped out of his skin.

"Don't worry son, it's only a rat," said Graves sounding rather rattled. "There's always a few of 'em in these old churches!"

Archer let out a cloud of foggy breath. "So the girl made the ghost sounds?" he asked.

"No one could prove nuffink."

"And the arsenic story – was that made up too?"

"Kent said so, but then he would."

Far above their heads the church clock struck midnight.

"It's getting late," said Archer.

Graves cleared his throat. "Begging your pardon, sir," he said "Are you sure you want to draw her? She's been dead a long while and I wouldn't fink your readers would like to see her if she's a bit … worm-eaten."

"We had better find out," said Archer grimly.

"Very good, sir," said Graves, standing up. "It's too perishing cold to sit much longer."

He fished in the pocket of his grubby apron and pulled out his screwdriver. Slowly and with much scraping, he undid the rusty fastenings and lifted the heavy wooden coffin lid. He reached into the coffin and gently pulled the cold dusty sheet from the dead woman's face.

Joe gulped and closed his eyes. He felt scared of ghosts. And what horrors they might find in the coffin.

"Well … I never!" gasped Graves.

Archer sucked in his breath. Slowly, Joe opened his eyes.

Fanny lay in her coffin with a peaceful expression on her beautiful face. Her eyes were closed and there were no smallpox scars on her cheeks.

"It looks like she's asleep," whispered Joe.

"I've never seen nuffink like this," muttered Graves. "Not once in 30 years."

Archer stared at the woman's face, taking in every detail.

"There's only thing that could have preserved her like this…" he said.

"It's arsenic, innit, sir?" said Graves quietly.

So maybe the ghost was telling the truth, thought Joe. He shuddered. But this time it wasn't the cold.

Two rotten arsenic rumours

1 Arsenic is said to preserve bodies by killing the germs that make the body decay. But some experts think that dry conditions may be more important in keeping germs at bay.

2 Arsenic may have been used by Japanese monks to turn their bodies into mummies … WHILE THEY WERE STILL ALIVE! What's that? You'd like to do this to your brother or sister (purely in the interests of science)? Well, don't let me stop you…

THE DIY JAPANESE MUMMY KIT

HERE'S WHAT YOU DO…

PUFF, PANT!

DAY 1 TO 1,000 — Live off nothing but nuts and seeds and enjoy happy healthy runs up mountains. This should get rid of all the fat on your body. (Fat makes the body rot quicker.)

CHOMP!

DAY 1,001 TO 2,000 — Eat only pine tree bark and pine needles. And don't forget to munch a bit of arsenic — it makes a tasty change from eating trees!

GLUG!

DAY 2,001 — Drink some more poison to kill the maggots after you die.

DAY 2,002 – Bury yourself alive without food or water in a nice dry tomb for three years.

BYE!

Three years later ...
CONGRATULATIONS!
You're now a genuine Japanese mummy.
Have a nice afterlife!

THANKS!

IMPORTANT ANNOUNCEMENT

We would like to apologize to readers who have ordered DIY mummy kits. They've been confiscated by the police. It's been against the law in Japan to make anyone into a mummy since 1895. And it's considered a very grave matter.

WHAT A SWIZ!

Well, I don't know about you – but all that talk about eating is making me hungry. And *not* for arsenic and pine needles! No, I fancy a nice big crunchy salad!

Ooh-er! I've peeped at the next chapter and I've changed my mind…

POP!

PAINFULLY POISONOUS PLANTS

How often have you heard this?

But the plants in this chapter are so VERY BAD for you that if you ate them you wouldn't just have green fingers – you'd probably be green all over. Time for a word of warning…

HORRIBLE HEALTH WARNING!

Are you listening? This is so important I'm going to say it twice. Don't Eat Wild Plants. I said,

DON'T EAT WILD PLANTS!

Even plants you think are safe could be poisonous! And make sure your brother, sister and pet rabbit get this message too.

And now for everything you ever wanted to know about poisonous plants in ten seconds – but only if you read this next bit *really* F-A-S-T!

DANGER! Poisonous plants fact attack

1 There are hundreds of poisonous plants – including many plants you eat!

2 They're poisonous because they want to stop bugs and animals from eating them as side salads.

SPOT THE POISONOUS PLANT!

3 The reason we're still alive is because we cook them first to destroy the poisons, or only eat the non-poisonous bits.

4 Some plants' poisons are deadly for bugs but not humans. Garlic, for example, makes slugs and snails ooze slime until they wither into slug mummies. Imagine your nose squirting snot until your body shrivels into something that lives in a pyramid!

5 Some poisonous plants are useful. In 1640, plant expert John Parkinson found out that mice won't eat books printed with ink containing poisonous wormwood juice. By the way, it's not very likely that this book is printed with poisonous ink, but don't let the dog chew it to find out.

6 Some plant poisons can be used as medicines…

• Digitalis (didge-it-ah-lis) is a drug that speeds up the heartbeat. It was first found as a poison in foxgloves.

• Curare (cu-rah-ray) comes from South American strychnos (strick-nos) vines. It's a nerve poison that stops signals getting to the muscles. The muscles can't move, so they relax – and that's handy for surgeons who need to operate on nice relaxed bodies.

• Atropine (at-rop-peen) comes from deadly nightshade. Like curare, atropine blocks nerve messages and relaxes muscles.

7 Some plants are irritating rather than deadly. Touch them and they'll make you sore – now that would be a little rash! Eat them and you'll get a sore mouth, but that would be even more stupid.

Bet you never knew!
The dumb cane of South and Central America gets its name because if you eat it you can't say a word. The poison in the leaves makes your mouth so sore you can't talk for hours. Mind you, you'd have to be pretty dumb to sample this unspeakable poison.

HOW CAN I HELP THIS IDIOT IF HE WON'T TELL ME WHAT HE'S EATEN?

CHOKE!

An irritating irritating-plants quiz
Which of these plants are irritating and which aren't?

Answers:
Sorry, readers, it's a trick quiz – they're ALL irritating!
Now isn't that an *irritating* result? Oh well, you can
always try it on your teacher!

a) Hot chillies irritate the mouth. Eat a few of them
and your face turns red and your eyes turn bloodshot.
But that doesn't stop strange people in Wisconsin,
USA, holding chilli-eating contests.

b) Celery-stem juice can sting your skin in sunlight.

c) Stinging nettles. Well, that was an easy one! Did you know that the nettles in the centre of a clump are said to sting less? These plants are older and their poison isn't as strong – but don't go bounding into clumps of nettles to find out!

d) Sorry, but pretty yellow buttercups are more like *bitter*-cups. Their juice can sting the skin.

e) Another DEAD giveaway. The sticky oily poison sticks to the skin. You can pick up the poison from clothes and it can even be carried in smoke on specks of ash. It's said that you can get a rash even by touching a dog that's been in contact with poison ivy. The Count has offered to test this idea using Gutzache and Watson...

Hmm – Gutzache doesn't seem *up to scratch*. Oh well, at least Watson's coat protected *him* from the poison.

So irritating plants can be a sore subject, but at least they don't kill people. Unlike the pizzas Donna Venoma cooks up...

Donna Venoma's
POISON PIZZA
COOKBOOK

I ALWAYS SERVE MY GUESTS THE FINEST PIZZA AND THEY NEVER COMPLAIN. IN FACT, THEY DON'T SAY MUCH AT ALL AFTER DINNER...

SPECIALITY MUSHROOM PIZZAS
(Just like my mama used to make before she got sent to prison!)

THE FLY AGARIC PIZZA
(It looks great and gets rid of flies too!)

ERK!

FLY AGARIC TOADSTOOLS (TASTEFUL RED COLOUR WITH WHITE SPOTS)

PARMESAN CHEESE AND ARSENIC DUSTED ON TOP

EEK!

PIZZA BASE

MOZZARELLA

THE DEATH-CAP SURPRISE PIZZA
(The surprise is how deadly it is — it's guaranteed to cause vomiting and liver failure!)

TOMATO (MAKE SURE YOU PUT IN A FEW POISONOUS BITS*)

DEATH-CAP TOADSTOOLS

GREEN OLIVES (TO MATCH THE COLOUR OF THE DEATH CAPS)

FRESHLY CHOPPED HEMLOCK LEAVES

EESH!

(OTHER INGREDIENTS AS BEFORE)

THE DESTROYING ANGEL SUPREME PIZZA
(Just as deadly as death cap)

DESTROYING ANGEL TOADSTOOLS (THEY LOOK LIKE ORDINARY MUSHROOMS BUT THEY'RE MUCH MORE FUN)

A FEW RED-HOT CHILLIES TO SPICE IT UP

UGH!?

* see page 88.

87

Hopefully the pizzas served in your school canteen aren't quite as deadly as these poison pizzas – but the canteen is a great place to torture a teacher (all in the interests of education, naturally!).

Teacher's lunchtime teaser

Your teacher is relaxing with a healthy school-dinner salad and a baked potato. Smile sweetly and say…

At this point your teacher might turn a colour of a ripe tomato (this is probably rage and not a sign of poisoning). If you're very brave you could point out…

IT'S TRUE, THE SPROUTING AND GREEN BITS OF THE POTATO ARE POISONOUS. SO ARE THE LEAVES. AND GUESS WHAT? TOMATO LEAVES AND STEMS ARE POISONOUS TOO! EATING THE WRONG BITS OF THESE PLANTS CAUSES DIARRHOEA AND BREATHING PROBLEMS!

Red for danger?

In 1820 many people in the USA believed that juicy red tomatoes were as poisonous as the rest of the plant. But a man named Colonel Robert Johnson had other ideas…

TOMATOES ARE GOOD FOR YOU.

SO PROVE IT!

VERY WELL, IN BOSTON, ON 26 SEPTEMBER, I WILL EAT A WHOLE BASKET OF TOMATOES!

BUT THAT'S A DEADLY DOSE!

EVERYONE THOUGHT THAT ROBERT WOULD DIE AND THOUSANDS TURNED UP TO WATCH...

IS HE EATING THEM WITH DRESSING?

YES, HE'S KEEPING HIS CLOTHES ON.

THE GREAT TOMAT

ROBERT ATE A TOMATO.

MMMM

ROBERT ATE 20 TOMATOES ... AND LIVED!

NOW HE'S SHOWING OFF.

SLURP!

MUNCH!

DO TOMATOES MAKE YOU RETCH UP?

CHOMP! CHEW!

GREAT TOMATO EATING DIS

NO, THEY MAKE YOU KETCHUP.

89

So there we are. The garden is gruesome, mushrooms are murderous and salads are sinister. But the very worst plant poisons are coming up right now. And when I say worst, I mean the really WORST!

Seven sinister plant products that you wouldn't want to sample in a salad

1 Castor-oil seeds. Eat the seeds and they'll probably pop straight through your guts and … you know the rest. But the actual poison – RICIN – is twice as deadly as a cobra's bite. It causes a burning mouth and blisters, bleeding guts and kidney failure.

2 Strychnos seeds. The same vicious vine that makes curare also brings you – STRYCHNINE. This painful poison attacks the nerves and stops them switching off after a signal passes along them. The muscles go mad. Victims end up arched over with a giant grin on their faces. And no, it's not because they're happy – it's all a result of the mad muscle twitches.

3 Henbane and deadly nightshade contain HYOSCINE. It's another nasty nerve poison, but this time the nerve signals get blocked at junctions between nerves and muscles. It's a bit like a traffic jam when the traffic lights break down. And the body breaks down too.

4 There's hyoscine in mandrake. This human-shaped root was supposed to scream when it was pulled up. The scream was said to kill all who heard it, so the Romans trained dogs to dig up the root.

5 Rhubarb contains OXALIC (ox-al-lick) ACID. It's used in dyeing (sorry, that's not a dire joke) and it also gets rid of unwanted stains and rust. But don't let that put you off rhubarb – the poison's only in the leaves.

6 Apricot kernel (seed). Apricots are fine but their kernels contain a deadly nerve poison called CYANIDE … and you can find out a bit more about cyanide in a moment. (If you're brave enough, that is!)

7 Aconite. Otherwise known as wolf's bane, it's a pretty white flower, but the effects of the poison are far from pretty. They include tingling and burning skin, followed by heart failure.

Bet you never knew!
In 1881, police suspected aconite had been used to murder a man but there was no scientific test to prove it. So scientist Dr Stevenson had to take fluid from the guts of the body and touch it with his tongue. Sure enough, the scientist felt tingling and pain for four hours. Oh well, at least he had the problem licked.

Painful poison fact file

NAME: Cyanide

THE BASIC FACTS: **1** Remember that ghastly hydrogen cyanide gas from page 54? Cyanide is a carbon and a nitrogen atom that get together to cause trouble.

2 They latch on to many types of atom, including sodium, hydrogen and potassium, to make poisons.

3 If cyanide gets in the body, it sticks to enzymes. Especially the enzyme needed to use oxygen to make energy.

4 So the effect of cyanide is the same as if the body can't breathe. The body weakens, the face turns blue and the heart stops.

THE PAINFUL DETAILS: **1** Now I really don't want you to panic about this – OK? Not only is there cyanide in apricot seeds, it's in apple and plum pips too!

EEK! OOER! YIKES!

2 I said, DON'T PANIC! You can eat a fruit salad safely! Even if you swallow a pip by mistake it will pass through your guts without harm. But eating an apricot seed can cause vomiting and breathing problems.

Millions of people in Africa eat cassava, a type of root that contains cyanide. The root came from Brazil, where native people made it safe by spitting on the root and leaving it to rot. Germs in the spit make enzymes that stop the poison working. But that's not an excuse to spit on your school dinner…

In Africa, people get rid of the poison by letting cassava rot in ponds. And although eating veg that's been mouldering in a smelly green pond doesn't sound like fun, it's much more jolly than a dose of cyanide.

But humans aren't the only animals that can eat some poisonous plants safely. Some creatures actually *enjoy* picnicking off poison! Goats happily dine off deadly nightshade and colorado beetles eat it all the time – even though it's heaving with horrible hyoscine. And some creatures eat poisons and store them in their body which makes them become poisonous too. Monarch butterfly caterpillars chomp their way through poisonous milkweed. The poison makes the caterpillars poisonous and they turn into poisonous butterflies. Other animals won't touch them.

Scientists aren't too sure how some creatures can eat poisons and live. But one thing is certain, monarch butterflies aren't the only lethal life forms around. The next chapter is *alive* with them…

APPALLINGLY POISONOUS ANIMALS

Say the word "animal" to your little sister and she'll probably say…

AHHHH!

She'll be thinking of cute kittens and playful puppies, of course. But if she saw the animals in this chapter she'd probably say…

ARRRRRRGH!!

There are hundreds of poisonous creatures. Like plants, they use poison to defend themselves from being eaten – but some, like spiders and snakes, use poison to catch animals to eat. And now let's pay a visit to Count Vomito's private zoo. He says visitors are always dying to see the animals – or is it dying *after* they've seen them?

THIS IS A BIG JOB!

AND WHEN YOU'VE FINISHED, THERE'S A PILE OF VISITORS THAT NEEDS CLEARING UP.

Queasy poison quiz

Here's a selection of creatures – which of them
ARE poisonous and which of them AREN'T?

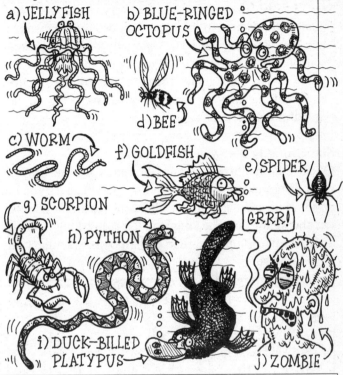

a) JELLYFISH

b) BLUE-RINGED
OCTOPUS

d) BEE

c) WORM

f) GOLDFISH

e) SPIDER

g) SCORPION

h) PYTHON

GRRR!

i) DUCK-BILLED
PLATYPUS

j) ZOMBIE

Answers:

a) Yes (see page 96).

b) Yes (see page 101).

c) No – so good news! You can eat as much worm
spaghetti as you like!

d) Yes (see page 103).

e) Yes (see page 107).

f) No, which is why the Count's cat is taking a close
interest in Bubbles the goldfish.

g) Yes (see page 107).

h) No, the python squeezes its victims to death – fancy a hug?

i) Yes, the male is one of a very few poisonous mammals. (Mammals are warm-blooded, furry creatures like you and your cat.) The dippy duck-bill has poison spurs on its legs and no one's too sure what they're for.

j) No, but some scientists reckon that zombies really exist and that they've been poisoned. We'll dig up the dreadful details later…

Something to give you the shakes

Of all the creatures in Count Vomito's private zoo, the most dangerous is the box jellyfish. So whatever you do, don't swim off the coast of Northern Australia between October and May. The stings on the metre-long tentacles are like microscopic murderous harpoons that inject tiny bags of poison.

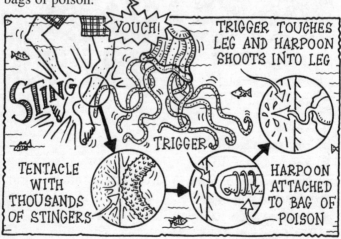

The painful poison can kill a man in just 120 SECONDS – it's enough to turn your legs into quivering jelly!

One victim, John Carrier, was stung in 1990. He said it felt like he'd walked into a "bush of flame". The pain is so violent many people drown because they forget to swim. Passer-by Peter Miller heard John's cry of pain and said it was…

> A horrible blood-curdling scream that went right through my body. It made my skin crawl.

But John was lucky! He hadn't been stung badly enough to die in seconds and an ambulance crew saved his life with a substance that stops the stings – vinegar.

And now for a rather painful question. What's even more painful than being stung by a jellyfish? Answer – being stung by a jellyfish *and* a fish. To find out more, let's take a look at the Count's fish tank. There are things in there that would give Bubbles the goldfish a heart attack…

NO TANKS!

Fearsome fish facts

There are about 30,000 types of fish, but only 250 are poisonous. Count Vomito is especially fond of his stonefish. They have poison spines to stop other fish eating them. It's nothing personal but they'll also stab anyone who treads on them by mistake. And it's easily done, because guess what? They look just like stones! (By the way, if you do tread on a stonefish the pain makes you froth at the mouth and roll around and bite anyone who comes near. The poison makes your leg swell up like an elephant's leg and your toes turn black and drop off. So tread carefully!)

Could you be a scientist?

You are working in a British oceanarium in 2001 and you've got a poison problem. Dottie the dicefish is feeling tense and squirting poison. How do you calm her down?

a) Play her a selection of relaxing music.

b) Give her a big toy dice to make friends with.

c) Stun her with an electric shock – BEWARE, you could be DICE-ing with death!

Answer: If you said **c)** be warned – it's extremely dangerous. And putting electrodes in your goldfish's bowl is a criminal offence! The answer is **b)!** Dottie was given a dice and, true to her name, daft Dottie decided the dice was her dad (or mum). Soon Dottie and her dice were deeply devoted. Would you make a mistake like this?

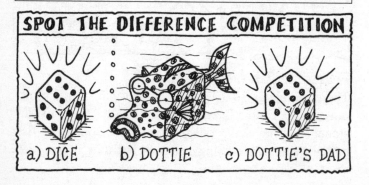

SPOT THE DIFFERENCE COMPETITION

a) DICE   b) DOTTIE   c) DOTTIE'S DAD

The perils of pufferfish

Pufferfish don't have poison spines, but parts of the pufferfish *are* poisonous – and they're 275 times more deadly than cyanide. The first sign of poisoning is tingling. Then you go numb and can't move and can't breathe. And there's NO antidote. But that doesn't stop people in Japan *eating* the non-poisonous bits. They're popular with people who enjoy dangerous dinners (so why don't they just eat school dinners – they're *really* risky!).

We needed someone to go undercover to sample the perilous pufferfish. But who was up to this scary job?

HEY I LOVE FISH – IT'S EASY MONEY!

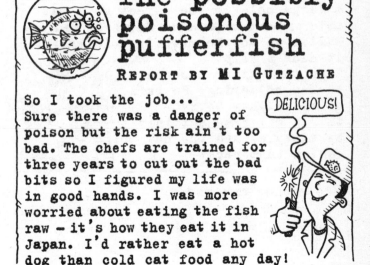

The possibly poisonous pufferfish

REPORT BY MI GUTZACHE

So I took the job...
Sure there was a danger of poison but the risk ain't too bad. The chefs are trained for three years to cut out the bad bits so I figured my life was in good hands. I was more worried about eating the fish raw – it's how they eat it in Japan. I'd rather eat a hot dog than cold cat food any day!

DELICIOUS!

So I sat in the restaurant and waited for the fish. I started thinking and I wished I hadn't. I'd done my homework and I knew that just 10 g of poisonous pufferfish can kill. Then the fish arrived. I was finally face-to-face with the fish. Could it be a fatal fish? Watson sniffed it and he kinda turned up his nose. Mind you, he ain't too keen on seafood.

I took a very small bite. It was enough, I figured. The fish tasted fishy. I began to sweat - would I die? I felt sick. It was the poison - I knew it! I cursed my luck. To think I'd survived organized crime to get puffed out by a pufferfish. I wanted out so I headed for the door. As luck would have it there was a large hole in the street so I was able to test an ancient Japanese remedy. Burial up to the neck in cold earth. It didn't help.

Then the waiter came out. He was hollering. He said he was mighty sorry — they'd given me sardines by mistake. And the cat wanted them back!

More seriously scary sea-life

If you're swimming off an Australian beach you've got more than killer jellyfish and fearsome fish to be scared of…

OK, so it may look cute but the blue-ringed octopus bites!

And its spit is deadly poison!

If you take it home as a pet you'll regret it for the rest of your life ... but that won't be long!

A bite from a blue-ringed octopus doesn't feel too bad. At first the bite doesn't hurt. But the octopus' spit contains a nasty nerve poison that makes you blind, throw up and lose control of your muscles. Death can follow in three hours.

And now for another creature that will put you off your seafood salad...

Could you be a scientist?

In the 1950s the CIA (the US secret service) had an embarrassing problem. They'd absent-mindedly lost enough poison to kill 110,000 people...

1 But the amazing thing is that this poison came from a rather tasty shellfish. Which one?

a) Scampi.

b) Starfish.

c) Clams.

2 Where did the poison turn up?

a) In a seafood soup served in the canteen.

b) A toilet.

c) A freezer.

3 What happened to the poison?

a) It was poured into an enemy leader's tea.

b) It was fed to 110,000 very unlucky hamsters.

c) It was given away free to scientists.

OOER!

Hmm – maybe we're safer on dry land... Or maybe not!

Bully bees and wicked wasps

Each year brutal bees and wicked wasps kill more than 40,000 people all over the world. Their stings aren't usually deadly but lots of people get stung and some victims are allergic (dangerously sensitive) to poison. They suffer heart attacks as a result of the shock.

Unlike wasps, bees die when they sting. Their stings have barbs like tiny harpoons and the bee can't yank them out of your skin. So the bee flies off leaving half its insides behind...

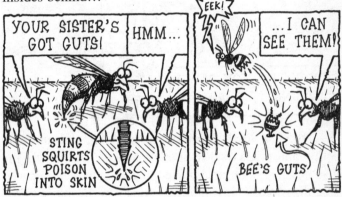

You'd think that would be enough to make bees think twice about stinging. And they do – but not all of them. African honeybees sting first and ask questions later. (Correction – they're too dead later to ask questions so they just sting.)

The buzz about bees

1 I bet you'd rather not know – but in 1964 a young Zimbabwean boy was stung 2,243 times by bees. He tried to hide from them in a river but the brutal bees stung him until his head turned black with stings and swelled up like a football. Amazingly he lived.

2 A scientist tried to find out how dangerous African honeybees really are. He juggled a ball in front of their hive to see how many times the ball got stung. But the bad-tempered bees attacked the stupid scientist instead. He was stung 92 times in a few seconds and ran 800 metres to get away. Sadly nobody clocked his time – it could have been a new world record.

3 In 1957, a South American scientist had a smart idea. Why not breed bad-tempered African bees with the friendly buzzy European bee? You'll get a well-behaved bee that does well in hot countries – well, that was the idea. But what they got was ... KILLER BEES! The bees escaped in Brazil and now they've spread to the USA.

Killer bees attack anything that goes near their hive and they like nothing better than nesting in people's houses. In fact, they'd like to move in with YOU!

EEK! OUCH! **BEEHIVE** YOURSELVES! YEOW! ARGH! OOF! ERK!

Bet you never knew!
One insect has poison that's even more painful than bee stings. I'm talking about the Spanish fly. It's a bit of a misleading name because this bug isn't a fly and it isn't always Spanish – it's a green beetle that also lives in France! The beetle's juice makes blisters on the skin and burns your insides if you swallow it. One victim threw up multi-coloured sick. (And no, it wasn't a new art form.)

Fancy making friends with a few more cruel creepy-crawlies? Well, tough, because they don't want to make friends with you!

Really revolting creepy-crawlies

It turns out that Count Vomito has a passion for centipedes, scorpions and spiders. He's got a special corner of his zoo where they live and he calls them his "willing little helpers", but I wouldn't like to think what they're helping him with. Anyway, he's promised to let us have a peek in his top-secret book of poisons…

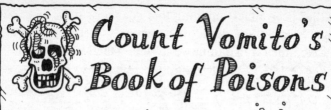

Count Vomito's Book of Poisons

NAME: Centipede

DESCRIPTION: 30–46 legs, body divided into segments. About 3,000 different types.

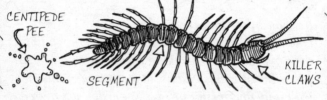

CENTIPEDE PEE

SEGMENT

KILLER CLAWS

WHERE FOUND: Damp, sheltered places all over the world.

HOW THEY POISON: Poison claws at front.

EFFECTS ON VICTIM: Kills millipedes, but only some types hurt humans. One variety that lives in the Philippine Islands can cause pain for three weeks — how fascinating!

POISONING POSSIBILITIES: Centipedes can live for a few hours in the human stomach. The poison causes sickness and breathing problems. Hmm — I wonder if anyone would like to try a cheese and centipede sandwich?

DEADLY STINGER

NAME: Scorpion

DESCRIPTION: Powerful pincers and eight legs. About 650 different types. GULP!

WHERE FOUND: Hot countries.

HOW THEY POISON: Sting on end of tail.

EFFECTS ON VICTIM: Kills small animals. Sadly, most scorpions aren't dangerous to humans. The most deadly is the centruroides scorpion that lives in Mexico and Arizona and kills one out of every hundred people it stings. And that means 15,000 deaths a year.

HEE HEE!

POISONING POSSIBILITIES: Scorpions hide in shoes and beds. I must put a few in the guest bedroom!

NAME: Spider

ABDOMEN   HEAD/CHEST   EYES

DESCRIPTION: Eight legs, body divided into a head/chest and abdomen, eight eyes. At least 32,000 different types — but probably thousands more await discovery. (Oh good! I hope they're deadly!) Their bodies measure between 0.5 mm and 9 cm long. They make good pets, too!

107

WHERE FOUND: All over the world including my bathroom, I'm pleased to say.

HOW THEY POISON: Poison fangs.

EFFECTS ON VICTIM: Stops victim escaping so it can be eaten at leisure. Only a few spiders are deadly to humans — the black widow of the USA, the wandering spider of Brazil and the funnel-web of Australia are examples. Unfortunately, most spiders can't bite through human skin and those that can, such as tarantulas, don't have a powerful enough poison to kill. It's all very frustrating!

@#!!!

BOG–STANDARD BLACK WIDOW

POISONING POSSIBILITIES: Black widow spiders hide under toilet seats and wandering spiders wander about the house. I think I feel an evil plot coming on!

So would you volunteer to be bitten by a black widow spider? If you think that sounds like a hairy situation you may be shocked to learn that in 1933 a Canadian scientist named Allan Blair actually let himself be bitten as an experiment!

But let's hear the spider's side of the story...

The Spider Magazine
1933

In this week's issue:
- THE GOOD WEB GUIDE
- FLY CUISINE
- I BIT A SCIENTIST ... AND LIVED

I BIT A SCIENTIST ... AND LIVED!

A black widow's heart-warming human-interest story. As told to Airey Legges

HI!

For years we spiders have lived in terror of humans trapping us in their baths and breaking our webs for fun. But now a brave black widow spider is biting back.

BZZZ!

I sure am. It all started with a scientist starving me for two weeks to make me bad-tempered...

So you were pretty mad?

BZZZ!

Not as mad as he was to let me bite his little finger!

So what happened to him?

ERK!

Well, the finger turned blue and red and then swelled up like a giant purple sausage. It was all very colourful. (And the things he was saying sounded even more colourful. But I'm a spider and I don't understand that kind of language!)

STAYING FOR DINNER, AIREY?

And now for a creepy bedtime story from *Poison Pen Tales* that will scare your little brother or sister's pants off. It helps if you read the story by torchlight and keep a toy spider hidden up your sleeve until the vital moment...

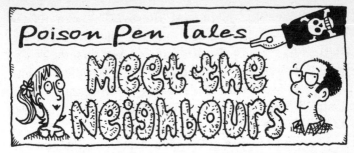

Meet the Neighbours

Meet Elbert and Wilma, a typical all-American couple who worked hard and saved up to achieve their ultimate dream: to build their very own home in sunny Arizona.

After years of saving, Elbert and Wilma had enough money. So they built their dream house and made ready to move in.

"Say, Elbert," said Wilma. "I figure there's one thing missing from our lovely new home."

"So what's that, my little patootie?" asked Elbert.

"Why, big huggy-bear, I'm talking about one of them big saguaro cactus things. I've always wanted one. And I figure it will look just fine in our living room!"

"Well, honey bunch," replied Elbert, "what are we waiting for? Let's get ourselves down to the garden centre and purchase one."

And so they did. And Wilma was right – the cactus did look good in the new living room.

Three weeks later Wilma and Elbert threw a house-warming party. All their friends and neighbours came,

111

even though the night was stormy. The rain fell in torrents and the thunder boomed and the lightning flashed like a crazy Christmas tree. And then the power failed. Everything went dark, but the guests didn't mind. The party went with an even bigger swing in the dark. Until Wilma saw something in the shadows … and SCREAMED!

Everyone stopped talking and stared. Laughter died in their throats. Their drinks dropped on to the new carpet.

Was it just the flickering lightning – or had the cactus come to life? Yes – there was no doubt. The giant plant was wiggling and wriggling as if it were dancing!

With trembling hands Elbert switched on his torch and pointed the light at it. And everyone began to scream at the tops of their voices. What they saw emptied the house in just 30 seconds.

The cactus was alive all right! It was alive … with *spiders.* Deadly, poisonous, biting baby tarantulas. Their mother had laid them as eggs in the cactus and now they had hatched. And the babies were hungry!

Hundreds of tarantulas were creeping and crawling over the carpet and climbing the curtains. They were scuttling over shoes, hiding in handbags and tiptoeing up trouser legs. They would bite anything that moved and their poison was four times more deadly than a big tarantula's.

(And that's when you quietly place the toy spider on your brother or sister and shout, WHAT'S THAT IN YOUR HAIR?!)

So how do you feel now? A bit green perhaps? Oh good, you'll be just the right colour to make friends with the Count's next group of poisonous pets...

Frightening frogs and toads

1 Frogs and toads have poison in their skin.

2 Some frogs go a little over the top in this area. The poison-arrow frog of Columbia, South America, is so dreadfully deadly that just 0.0001 g of its poison can kill.

3 And that means that (help ... where's my calculator?) a yoghurt pot full of poison (weighing 28.3 g) could kill 2.5 million people! That's some frog.

4 In the 1970s scientists discovered the South American terrible frog. The poison from this frog is so deadly that the scientists had to wear rubber gloves to touch it. When a chicken and a dog touched the gloves they died.

5 If frogs are frightening, toads can be terrifying. A dog that chews a toad will throw up and foam at the mouth. It could die.

113

But there's one creature that makes even the most poisonous frog or toad look like a harmless happy hopper. On a scale of one to ten, this scaly beast is right off the scale…

Scary poisonous snakes

So how would you like your very own poisonous snake pet? Of all the creatures in his private poison zoo, Count Vomito's favourite is his pet rattlesnake…

RATTLE!

SNAKES WILL ONLY ATTACK PEOPLE IF THEY'RE UPSET. I'M TRYING TO TRAIN SLIPPY, BUT HE'S EASILY RATTLED!

And now for some slippery snake secrets…

Painful poison fact file

NAME: Poisonous snakes

THE BASIC FACTS: **1** There are 2,300 types of snake, but only 300 are poisonous to people.

2 As Count Vomito says, no poisonous snake makes a habit of harming humans for no reason. They much prefer biting a juicy mouse or a tender baby bird. But we have an unfortunate habit of treading on them. And the snakes have an even more unfortunate habit of giving us free poison in return.

3 Snakes inject poison through hollow fangs or along grooves in their fangs. The poison is made in special glands on the sides of the head.

JAB!

SQUIRT!

X-RAY VIEW OF POISON IN A FANG

X-RAY VIEW OF SNAKE'S SKULL

THE PAINFUL DETAILS: You've got similar glands on the side of your head, but they just make spit. (And luckily human spit isn't poisonous, or teachers who spray spit when they talk would kill off half their classes.)

THE SPITTING COBRA—AN ESPECIALLY POISONOUS SPECIES!

Different snakes produce different poisons and some are more deadly than others. You can imagine them as different "flavours" and Count Vomito has just made two of them into milkshakes…

| Extra-strong strawberry and nerve-poison flavour from real green mambas — stops you moving for ever! | Blackcurrant and blood-dripping flavour from rattlesnakes — makes the blood leak from your blood vessels, so your cells can't get enough oxygen... and die. |

But if snakes can be sinister, humans can be even more horrible. In the southern states of the USA, there are festivals called "rattlesnake round-ups". Thousands of innocent snakes are killed during these cheery celebrations. The story goes that one rattlesnake rounder-upper used to grab rattlesnakes by their tails and crack them like whips until their heads flew off. One day a head flew off … and bit him. He died.

HE WAS SO DARN PROUD OF THAT TRICK!

YEP! I GUESS IT WENT TO HIS HEAD

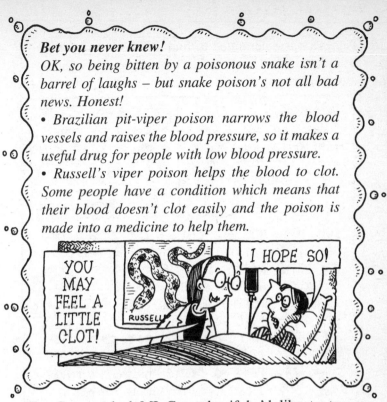

The Count asked MI Gutzache if he'd like to try a snakebite and tell us what it's like. But after thinking about it for half a second, Gutzache made up his mind…

NO WAY, PAL!

Strange snake scientists

Mind you, one strange scientist really did take snake poison. Dr F Eigenberger spent the 1920s injecting his body with snake poison to find out the painful effects.

And he was determined to find out the truth … even if it killed him. Here's what his notebook might have looked like…

Wednesday
Today I injected myself with green-mamba poison.

GREEN MAMBA

OOOOCH! My skin is itching and I've got a burning pain. Eh? Everything sounds strange. My neighbour's car sounds like it's got a flat tyre. I feel drunk - and that's odd, because I haven't touched a drop! Oh yuk! I feel sick. My eyes are sore and my face is numb. I can't feel my fingers and toes - have they dropped off?! Phew! No, they're still there, but now I can hardly breathe. Er - maybe it was a bad idea to take that poison!

Six hours later
I'm in agony. I'm dying, this is a most interesting scientific experience. Oh well, goodbye, cruel world!

Next day
Well, fancy that - I'm still alive! I'm sitting up in bed. I'm still a bit groggy but I'm over the worst. Great, I can try another experiment. Now where did I put that cobra poison?

Hmm, it sounds like the dodgy doc was one test tube short of a rack. But the most shocking thing about the test is that he weakened the poison *ten times* before he used it! If he'd tried it at full strength, it would have been exit Eigenberger.

Others weren't so lucky. In 1921, snake-show entertainer Tom Wanless was bitten by a green mamba. The next morning Tom looked really rough and was coughing up blood. He dragged himself over to the mirror and remarked...

THE GREEN MAMBA WINS!

Then he dropped down dead.

What Tom Wanless and Dr Eigenberger needed was a substance that could stop the snake poison working. In other words, an antidote – or anti-venom as it's known. And you'll be delighted to hear that snakebite antidotes actually exist...

Painful poison fact file

NAME: Anti-venom

THE BASIC FACTS: **1** Snake poisons are proteins. When the body detects the poison, it tries to fight it by making its own proteins called antibodies.

2 The job of the antibodies is to latch on to the poison proteins and clump them together so they can't do any harm.

3 Trouble is, in a fatal bite there's too much poison and it works too fast for the body to make enough antibodies.

EH?

4 If the body survives, it keeps some antibodies. And they can be useful if the person gets bitten again.

5 Scientists make anti-venom by injecting horses or sheep with small amounts of snake poison and taking the antibodies they make.

THE POISON IS COLLECTED BY MAKING THE SNAKE BITE INTO PLASTIC FILM

THE VENOM DRIPS INTO A JAR

THE PAINFUL DETAILS: But scientists need snake poison to give to the horses or sheep. And that means catching live deadly dangerous poisonous snakes. Anyone want to have a go? Thought not.

HEE HEE!

One person who did want to have a go was Australian snake expert Kevin Budden. Back in 1950, scientists needed to get hold of a live taipan from northern Australia to make an anti-venom. So Budden set off for Cairns to find one. But things went terribly wrong…

CAIRNS CHRONICLE ☼ 1950

BITE BEATS BRAVE BUDDEN!

We're sorry to report the death of Kevin Budden. Courageous Kev, 20, found a taipan under some stones. But before the young snake expert could bag the slippery stinger, it wrapped itself around his hands.

Kev needed expert help to free himself, so he asked passing truck driver Jim Harris to take him to the home of snake expert, Mr Stephens. Said Jim, "I'd never given a lift to a killer snake before but I wasn't going to argue!"

J. Harris

At Stephens' house Kev was again trying to bag the taipan when it bit him. He died the following day.

But Kevin Budden's death wasn't in vain. Scientists used the snake's poison to make the first-ever taipan anti-venom.

And now for our next painful chapter – er hold on, a reader wants to say something…

BUT YOU WERE GOING TO TELL US ABOUT ZOMBIES!

OOPS, sorry, silly me! Amazingly, some scientists think that zombies really exist and that people can become zombies by drinking poison. In 1980 a man named

Clairvius knocked on his sister's door in Haiti. Nothing odd about that except that Clairvius had been dead and buried for 18 years! He said that he'd been dug up and worked as a zombie slave by a voodoo priest.

US scientist Wade Davies heard the story and headed to Haiti in search of the truth. He paid a priest to let him in on a few trade secrets and found out how to make a zombie. Would you like to give it a go? Thought so!

THE DIY ZOMBIE KIT

NOW YOU CAN TURN YOUR BROTHER OR SISTER INTO A ZOMBIE SLAVE IN THE COMFORT OF YOUR OWN HOME!

All you need is...

A brother or sister

Our special top-secret zombie poison mix, which includes real genuine baby bones and pufferfish poison.

All you do is...

Give your brother or sister some poison (not too much now — you don't want to really kill them!)

DON'T WORRY, IT'S DELICIOUS!

With the right dose, your victim appears dead and gets buried. Then, all you have to do is dig them up and put them to work tidying your room and doing your science homework!

So there's NO WAY you'll be trying this at home? Well, I'm glad to hear that because it saves me the bother of telling you that there may be a law against poisoning members of your family and using them as slaves. And anyway most scientists aren't too sure that the zombie poison recipe was genuine.

So what do you think? Was Wade Davies told a load of voodoo-hoodoo? And would you be brave enough to find out the painful truth? If so, you could become a budding poison detective ... but you'll need to investigate the next chapter to be sure...

HOW TO BE A POISON DETECTIVE

Welcome to the Horrible Science Poison Detective Training Course! Your mission is to become a completely clued-up poison detective by the end of this chapter!

Lesson 1: Find out where poisons are kept

We sent MI Gutzache (now fully recovered from his embarrassing experience in the fish restaurant) to check out this perfectly normal house…

SO YOU JUST WANT ME TO CHECK OUT THE SCENE FOR POISONS?

THE HOUSE

AND I DON'T HAVE TO EAT NO FISH?

SURE I'LL TAKE THE JOB!

C'MON, WATSON, IT'S EASY MONEY!

GROAN!

The poison house mystery

REPORT BY MI GUTZACHE

So I got hired. It was my first bad move. I figured I knew the score – Watson could sniff out the poisons and I'd finger the greenbacks. We'd done it a thousand times but I didn't know the half of it. For one thing, I reckoned without the cat. Now don't get me wrong, cats are OK in their place – but that place is Mars. I know Watson shares my feelings...

BUT SHE'S ONLY A KITTEN!

HISS! SNARL!

After the kitty had been locked up, we continued our search. It was soon clear that the job was no cinch. The house contained more poison than Peter Popov's Poison Pepperoni Pizza Parlour – I mean the whole place was a danger zone! We came out with a box-load and we had to go back for more. Here's our haul...

1 COFFIN MIXTURE

2 BUGOFF

3 STICKIT

4 GOOD HAIR DAY

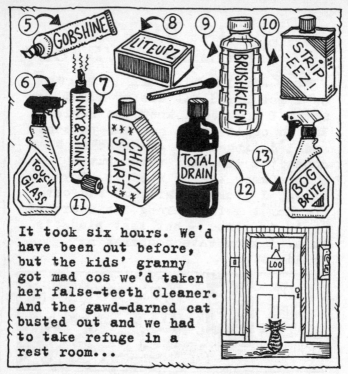

It took six hours. We'd have been out before, but the kids' granny got mad cos we'd taken her false-teeth cleaner. And the gawd-darned cat busted out and we had to take refuge in a rest room...

Let's take a closer look at what Gutzache found...

1 MEDICINES. All medicines and pills are poisonous in too-large doses. And so are denture-cleaning tablets.

2 INSECT AND WEED KILLERS are designed to kill pests and weeds. But they can also kill human pests and weedy people too.

3 The only safe GLUE is labelled safe for children. Most modelling glue or superglue could bring a person to a sticky end.

4 Things like WASHING-UP LIQUID, WASHING POWDER, SHAMPOO, SHOWER GEL and BUBBLE BATH aren't good to eat. You'd better not swallow any if you want a clean bill of health.

5 MOUTHWASH, DEODORANT and TOOTHPASTE are fine on the bits of body they're designed for, but you wouldn't want them for dinner.

6 GLASS CLEANERS and WINDOW CLEANERS may contain harmful chemicals. Breathing the mist from a spray can be *very* dangerous.

7 FELT-TIP PENS. The only safe ones are marked safe for children. Their ink is water-based. The ink in "smelly" felt-tip pens may contain harmful chemicals that could cause breathing problems and turn your skin blue if you breathed them in too much.

8 MATCHES. Strike-anywhere matches (the type that don't need to be struck on a matchbox) are poisonous if sucked. And only stupid suckers suck safety matches – they can cause an upset stomach.

9 TURPENTINE and WHITE SPIRIT are very poisonous. Two hundred years ago, doctors gave turps to patients with bladder stones. Some of them got tombstones instead.

10 PAINT STRIPPERS. Don't touch them or breathe their fumes. They're designed to strip paint but they're pretty good at stripping skin too.

11 ANTIFREEZE is scary stuff. Antifreeze reacts with body chemicals to make oxalic acid. So you get all the rotten results of rhubarb-leaf poisoning without eating rhubarb.

12 DRAIN CLEANERS and OVEN CLEANERS are good at dissolving those stubborn bits of burnt food. And good at dissolving stubborn people who ignore the warnings on the containers.

13 TOILET CLEANERS and BLEACH kill germs, *and* people if they try to drink them.

Well, that's the end of your first lesson, but before we start Lesson 2, you may like to know that drain, oven and toilet cleaners damage the skin because they're alkaline. And here are the painful details…

Everything you need to know about alkaline poisons
1 Alkaline chemicals are dissolved in water. The more water there is, the weaker the chemical, as the Count is about to show us…

2 The atoms in an alkaline chemical pull hydrogen atoms away from any other substance they come in contact with.
3 As it loses hydrogen atoms, the other substance dissolves. And you would dissolve too if you had a bath in drain cleaner.

But now for some good news: if you're wondering how alkaline chemicals are made, we've persuaded an oven cleaner to spill the beans (and clean them up again).

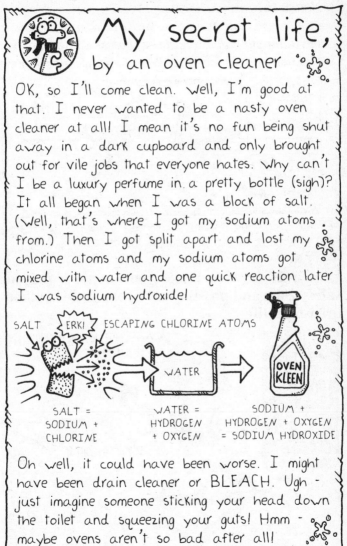

My secret life,
by an oven cleaner

OK, so I'll come clean. Well, I'm good at that. I never wanted to be a nasty oven cleaner at all! I mean it's no fun being shut away in a dark cupboard and only brought out for vile jobs that everyone hates. Why can't I be a luxury perfume in a pretty bottle (sigh)? It all began when I was a block of salt. (Well, that's where I got my sodium atoms from.) Then I got split apart and lost my chlorine atoms and my sodium atoms got mixed with water and one quick reaction later I was sodium hydroxide!

SALT — ERK! ESCAPING CHLORINE ATOMS

WATER

OVEN KLEEN

| SALT =
SODIUM +
CHLORINE | WATER =
HYDROGEN
+ OXYGEN | SODIUM +
HYDROGEN + OXYGEN
= SODIUM HYDROXIDE |

Oh well, it could have been worse. I might have been drain cleaner or BLEACH. Ugh - just imagine someone sticking your head down the toilet and squeezing your guts! Hmm - maybe ovens aren't so bad after all!

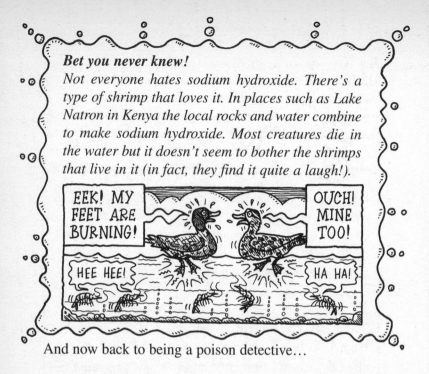

EEK! MY FEET ARE BURNING!

OUCH! MINE TOO!

HEE HEE!

HA HA!

And now back to being a poison detective…

Lesson 2: How to make your home a poison safety zone and possibly save your little brother or sister's life

You will need:

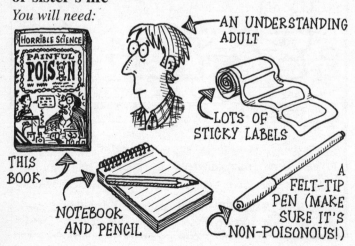

HORRIBLE SCIENCE
PAINFUL POISON

THIS BOOK

AN UNDERSTANDING ADULT

LOTS OF STICKY LABELS

NOTEBOOK AND PENCIL

A FELT-TIP PEN (MAKE SURE IT'S NON-POISONOUS!)

What you do:

1 Ask permission for this activity and make sure your baby brother or sister and pet hamster are under lock and key first. We don't want them sampling any poisons you find.

2 Draw a skull and crossbones poison logo on your sticky labels. Here's an arty one for you to copy – thanks, Tony!

3 Tour your home putting stickers on any poisons you find – you'll be amazed by how many stickers you need!

4 Make a note of any poison dangers you discover such as…

• Poisons or medicines that have been poured into different bottles.

HORRIBLE HEALTH WARNING!

This is SHOCKING! Just imagine trying to shampoo your hair with oven cleaner or taking paint stripper for a ticklish cough. If your family put poisons in different bottles, it's best to ring up social services and book yourself into a children's home. It's safer!

- Poisons stored in low-level unlocked cupboards that hungry little brothers and sisters and hamsters might get at.
- Poisons with lids that little kids can take off easily.
- Medicines kept in low cupboards that aren't locked.
- Poisons in leaking containers.

5 Report any dangers to the adult and suggest they take action. The best place for poisons is locked away out of reach of troublesome toddlers.

IMPORTANT MESSAGE!
The third part of your training is advanced high-level stuff and you may want to leave it until you get a job with the police.

Lesson 3: Dig up a poisoned body for tests

IMPORTANT NOTE!
Make sure you ask permission before digging up bodies. You wouldn't want to be chased around a graveyard by a vicious vicar, would you? And don't go digging up departed family pets to test your skills! Let Harry the hamster rest in peace!

VICIOUS VICAR

1 Put up a canvas screen around the grave. A seaside windbreak will do just so long as it isn't covered in silly cartoon characters in bright cheery colours.

THAT'S GROSS! YUK!

UGH, PUTRID!

2 Check to make sure you're digging up the right grave. It might be a bit embarrassing if you dig up the wrong body by mistake!

3 Open the coffin a bit to let the smelly gases out. (Put a clothes peg over your nose first.)

4 Don't forget to collect some earth from the grave. There might already be poisons in the soil that could affect your tests.

5 Take the coffin with the body in it away for further tests. It really is that easy (NOT)!

Lesson 4: Test the body for poisons

Besides the earth you collected from the grave, you're going to need samples (small amounts) of body to test. Here's a quick list…

SAMPLES FROM THE BODY TO TEST FOR POISON

STOMACH

LIVER

KIDNEYS

← POO

BLOOD   WEE

TEETH*

←BONES*

←HAIR*

USEFUL TOOLS FOR COLLECTING BODY SAMPLES

DAD'S PENKNIFE

MUM'S TROWEL

SISTER'S TWEEZERS

*GOOD PLACES TO LOOK IF THE POISON HAS BUILT UP OVER TIME.

But before we try some poison tests you might like to know who got the science of poison testing off the ground…

Hall of Fame: Mathieu Orfila (1787–1853)
Nationality: Spanish (later French)

The scientist faced a painful choice. Should he get involved in a murder enquiry?

Factory owner Charles Lafarge was dead. His wife Marie was on trial for murder and the court wanted to know if she'd used arsenic. Marie had bought arsenic rat killer but the police could find no trace of the poison in Charles' body. Orfila was the greatest poison expert in France – if anyone could find the poison he could. But if he got it wrong his enemies would crow louder than a crowd of cockerels. And an innocent woman could be executed.

MAYBE I'D BETTER THINK ABOUT IT.

IT WASN'T ME!

R.I.P. MARIE LAFARGE

Young Mathieu had studied medicine in Spain and he was such a good doctor the city of Barcelona gave him some money for more study. And that's how he came to

Paris. In 1814, Mathieu produced a brilliant book about poisons, full of painful details about what they do to the body and how to detect poisons in bodies. So he was the ideal person to solve the mystery death of Charles Lafarge.

Mathieu tried a test that had been invented just four years before, in 1836. It worked. The test proved that Lafarge had been killed by arsenic and Marie was found guilty. She was locked up for life and Orfila went on to carry out poison experiments on 4,000 unfortunate dogs. He founded a whole new science of poisons, which, if you want to sound dead scientific, is now known as toxicology (toxy-col-o-gy).

I'd like to say Mathieu Orfila lived happily ever after, but he didn't. After a revolution in 1848, the scientist didn't get on with the new government. He was no longer invited to top parties and offered top jobs. The stress made him ill and he died five years later. Today few people remember him or even know where he's buried. But at least no one's dug him up yet.

And that reminds me, we were supposed to be testing the body for poisons. Well, it helps if you have some whizzy equipment – so here are a few ideal presents for all you budding toxicologists!

COUNT VOMITO'S POISON PRODUCTS

proudly present...

Everything for the well-equipped poisons lab

ON SPECIAL OFFER THIS WEEK...

THIN-LAYER CHROMATOGRAPHY* KIT

It's easy-peasy! You dissolve your sample in a chemical and dip the paper in it. The sample soaks upwards and the poisons separate out. This test detects 90% of all known poisons!

*That's cro-ma-tog-graf-fee

DISSOLVE!

MASS SPECTROMETER

Use a powerful magnet to separate poison chemicals in a gas. It's something to gas about with your scientist friends.

I'M GETTING ONE FOR MY BIRTHDAY!

IMMUNOASSAY

Add the poison to other chemicals to make it fairly safe and inject it into an animal. The animal makes antibodies that you can test to show you what the poison was. (Animals not supplied.)

AND I'M NOT VOLUNTEERING!

What's that? You're not old enough for advanced detective work but you're itching to try some poison tests right now? Oh all right, here's a special experiment you can practise your skills on…

Dare you discover … how to test for poisons using paper chromatography?

You will need:
Some newspaper
A ruler
A strip of kitchen towel or blotting paper 5 cm wide and 20 cm long
Some green food colouring
A small paintbrush
A large pudding basin with 2 cm of water

What you do:
1 This is a messy experiment, so put down some newspaper or the next tests might be on *your* dead body.
2 Use the paintbrush to paint a blob of food colouring 0.5 cm across and 3 cm from one end of one of your paper strip.
3 Dip the first 1 cm of the paper strip into the water and lay it over the edge of the basin.

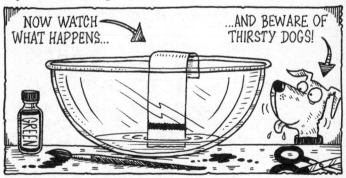

NOW WATCH WHAT HAPPENS…

…AND BEWARE OF THIRSTY DOGS!

GREEN

You should notice:

The water soaks upwards. When the water reaches the food colour, other colours begin to separate out. (It takes a few minutes to happen.) You can imagine painful poisons oozing out of a sinister sample. Why not experiment with different food colourings and water-based felt-tip pens?

CONGRATULATIONS! You've nearly finished this book! But can you remember the painful details? Well, here's your chance to find out if you're a dazzling detective or a bumbling boffin. This quiz is based on facts you've just read about. If you know the info, you can solve the mysteries!

Painful poison quiz
1 In 1838 a wicked wife in Germany tried to poison her husband. She made him a nice hot soup containing phosphorus. What made him suspicious?
a) The soup smelled of toilet cleaner.
b) The soup carried on bubbling even after it went cold.
c) The soup glowed in the dark.

2 In 1954 two women were poisoned by Spanish-fly juice. How did scientist Dr Lewis Nickells prove what poison was involved?
a) He heated it until it exploded.
b) It turned his pet rabbit into a zombie.

c) He put some of the victim's vomit on his arm and it made a blister.

3 Scarlet macaws are a type of parrot that live in South America. They live off seeds and fruit, including some poisonous plants. Why don't they end up as sick as parrots?
a) They eat clay afterwards.
b) They get monkeys to test the fruit first.

c) They store the poisons in their fantastic feathers.

4 In 1953 Clare Luce, the US ambassador to Italy, had it all – a top job, a palace to live in, servants to look after her and a lovely old painted ceiling to admire. Then she fell ill with a mysterious illness. She suffered from sickness and diarrhoea, her hair started to fall out, she felt dizzy and she said she saw a flying saucer. A doctor found arsenic in Mrs Luce's wee. Who was poisoning her?
a) Aliens.
b) The ceiling.
c) The doctor.

It's frightening, isn't it? There you are sitting in your palace drinking a lovely cup of coffee … and the ceiling is plotting to kill you! It shouldn't be allowed! There's no doubt – poisons are the most painful, scary chemicals ever … or are they?

Are you ready to face up to the PAINFUL truth?

EPILOGUE: THE PAINFUL TRUTH

OK, so it's 100% official – poisons are painful. And if you've just read this book then you won't need reminding of how painful poisons can be … but if you have forgotten, Count Vomito will be happy to remind you…

TAKE A SIP OF THIS AND YOU'LL NEVER FORGET ANYTHING, **EVER** AGAIN!*

As you'll be dead!

And because poisons are painful and deadly and dangerous – they're scary. So it's not too surprising that people like Sultan Abdul Hamid were terrified of poisons. And while we're on the subject, here's someone else who was scared of them…

Welcome to the TV show where we interview famous people about how they died!

This week we talk to King Mithradates VI (died 63 BC).

THIS IS YOUR **DEATH!**

I guess the story of King Mithradates VI may hold a lesson for us. It's easy to be scared of poisons – but there are even more scary things out there. Like cruel human enemies.

And if you think about it, should we really be scared of poisons? After all…

• Some poisons can be made into life-saving medicines – just think of those ever-so-valuable plant poisons and snake venoms. Thanks, guys!

*You're welcome

• Some poisons can be useful in industry. OK, so you wouldn't want to drink an arsenic and lead fizzy drink. But if it wasn't for the arsenic and lead in solder the author couldn't have typed this book on his computer.

• Some substances are poisonous if you take too much of them. But in smaller doses they're vital for life. Anyone fancy a sugar lump, a glass of water or a puff of oxygen? Well, if you don't have some soon, you'll be hungry, thirsty and gasping!

It's easy to feel scared by all those thousands of poisonous plants and animals or the poisons lurking in your kitchen cupboard. But even the most painful poison, such as cyanide, is only really scary if it's used as a weapon. If it falls into the wrong hands – the hands of people who use poison for killing and murder.

So the best way to deal with poisons isn't to be scared of them. It's to learn about poisons so you can protect yourself. You see, science is about more than making new chemicals – it's about using them safely and wisely too. Happy Horrible Science, everyone!

(DON'T WORRY – IT WAS ONLY A GLASS OF HEALTHY BRUSSELS SPROUT JUICE!)